W9-CTQ-576

LAS VEGAS GUIDE

ED KRANMAR AND AVERY CARDOZA

OPE

OPEN ROAD PUBLISHING, publisher of the **Passport Press Travel Series**, offers travel guides to American and foreign locales. Our books tell it like it is, often with an opinionated edge, and our experienced authors always give you all the information you need to have the trip of a lifetime. Write for your <u>free</u> catalog of all our titles, including our golf and restaurant guides.

OPEN ROAD PUBLISHING
P.O. Box 11249, Cleveland Park Station, Washington, DC 20008

*This book is dedicated to the Shuffler, the Doubler,
and to Grandma Kranmar*

First Edition

ACKNOWLEDGEMENTS
The authors would like to gratefully acknowledge the following people whose invaluable information helped make this a better book: the folks at *Las Vegas News Agency*; Karen, Mike, and Myram of the *Las Vegas News Bureau;* Howard Schwartz of the Gamblers Book Club; and the many anonymous Vegans who provided advice and tips over the years.

Photos courtesty of Las Vegas News Bureau
and Las Vegas Convention and Visitors Authority

nnot assume
uide; for any
r any reason.

TABLE OF CONTENTS

MAPS AND SIDEBARS

MAPS

SIDEBARS

1. INTRODUCTION

Las Vegas is America's most exciting city, and in this book we'll show you all that this great town has to offer. If you follow our advice, and we have plenty of it, you'll have the time of your life!

Of course, Vegas is built around gambling, but the city that never sleeps is much more. It's good, clean fun for families with its theme parks and video arcades, and it's also *Sin City* and topless numbers in the big casino production shows. It's a fun raft trip on Lake Mead, it's a breathtaking hike in Valley of Fire State Park, and it's also a visit to the "Eighth Wonder of the World" - monumental Hoover Dam.

We'll show you unexplored Las Vegas; where to go Country and Western dancing; how to rediscover Elvis and Liberace; and where to find delicious 99¢ shrimp cocktails. You'll find out where to go to enjoy some of the country's finest golfing, tennis, boating, and swimming, and if solitude and nature is desired, where to go to explore one's soul in the vast magnitude of the desert.

For people who never sleep or love to gamble, Vegas is paradise. While other travel guides may tell you how to play, we'll show you how to *win*. Armed with Avery Cardoza's inside tips, you'll learn everything you need to know to win money gambling.

It all adds up to excitement and thrills. We'll show you all the possibilities to help make your trip to Vegas one of the best you've ever taken!

NEVADA/SOUTHWEST MAP

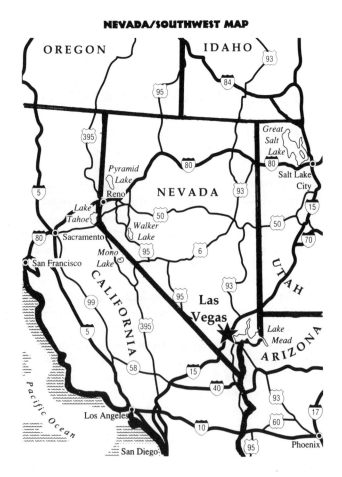

2. EXCITING LAS VEGAS!
- OVERVIEW -

Few cities in the world have the kind of hard-charging excitement and limitless possibilities that Las Vegas has, and the Entertainment Capital does it without breaking a sweat. We'll give you a quick preview here of all that Vegas has in store, so you can see how to plan your vacation and get the maximum enjoyment from it.

GAMBLING

You can gamble day or night, 24 hours - the casinos never close. With over 50 casinos in the immediate vicinity, and no lack of action in any of them, the gambler will find non-stop excitement.

Sit down at any table, and you've got action. In our gambling chapter, we'll show you how to play and win at blackjack, craps, poker, roulette, slots, video poker and keno, and most of all, how to walk away from the tables a winner.

HOTELS

Of the 13 largest resorts in the world, Las Vegas boasts 12 of them. Best of all, you'll get tremendous value pretty much wherever you stay. Casinos lure players to their premises by offering inexpensive rooms and food, and you'll benefit with excellent values on your lodging. They figure, and generally correctly, that their guests are a captive audience for their casino games. If you're a gambler, be sure to follow our money-management tips.

GAMBLING MANIA

*People will gamble on anything in this town: a hole of golf, or even how many french fries will be in their cup. There's almost nothing that brings in more **high-rollers** than the marquee boxing fights, where big gamblers come from around the world paying hundreds and even thousands of dollars for seats at these gala events, where millions of dollars are bet on the fate of one gladiator outlasting another. The gambling can even get out of hand: in the early 1980's employees at a local hospital were accused of betting on how long their terminal patients would live. Now that's really bizarre, even for Vegas.*

On the Strip, you'll find the ultra-chic **Mirage**, with its overflowing Volcano, Siberian tigers, and lush rainforest; the **Excalibur**, with its medieval theme featuring knights in shining armor; you can go back to ancient Rome in **Caesars Palace** and see the magnificent changing sky inside **Caesars Forum** shops; take a Nile River boat ride inside a 20th century pyramid in the **Luxor Hotel** (opening October 1993); or ride the water flume or indoor roller coaster behind **Circus Circus** in the new **Grand Slam Canyon**. Check out the **MGM Grand Hotel and Theme Park**, and they mean Grand! Opening in February 1994, it will be the world's biggest resort-casino at 5,009 rooms. Wow!

Downtown, Glitter Gulch lights up the sky at night with the most incredible display of neon you've ever seen. You'll find the famed **Binion's Horseshoe Casino**, not only home of the World Championship of Poker, a place where legends are born and also die, but also a place known to accept any bet, no matter the amount. And don't overlook the **Golden Nugget**, the class of Downtown, with some of the best dining in Vegas and the largest gold nugget on public display in the world. You'll also find a number of smaller, more down-to-earth casinos Downtown.

FOOD

Not only is the gambling non-stop, so is the food. At any time, day or evening, you can satiate your appetite with a $1.99 T-bone steak at 3:00 am, a $6.00 lunch buffet offering you a hundred items to choose from, or great 99¢ shrimp cocktails at the **Golden Gate Hotel and Casino**. Buffets are inexpensive and plentiful, but there's lot's of other great dining too, from ethnic eateries like **Chin's** fine Szechuan repasts to the massive, delicious steaks Vegas is known for (check out **William B's** at the Stardust or **The Steak House** at Circus Circus).

SHOWS

Vegas is entertainment, and some of the best shows in the world can be found right here. Lavish, often sexy shows featuring magic, acrobatics, comedy, singing and scantily-clad, gorgeous dancers will enthrall you.

The long-running **Siegfreid and Roy** show, the most popular show in town, will amaze and astound you with dazzling magic, white tigers, and more. Watch the Titanic sink on stage at Bally's **Jubilee!** show, or see the sensuous dancing at the Trop's **Folies Bergere**. A little out of the ordinary, Kenny Kerr's outrageous female impersonation show, **Boylesque**, is lots of fun. We'll give you the lowdown on these and other fantastic shows.

FAMILY ENTERTAINMENT

Despite what you might think, Vegas is a great place for kids. Swim and splash in one of the world's most fun water parks, **Wet 'n Wild**. Visit the must-see **Magic Motion Machines** at Excalibur - a simulated movie theater experience, where the seats are on hydraulic pumps and you feel like you're really on a runaway train. Whoa!!

Any visit to Vegas with kids has to include **Circus Circus**, with its high-wire and other circus acts, carnival games, an extensive video arcade, and the new Grand Slam Canyon, with its water rides and roller coasters.

How about the new **Treasure Island** (opening October 1993), where every hour on the hour pirates stage mock battles on the great ocean they call the Strip; the **Luxor** (opening October 1993) will transport you back to the days of Tut and Cleopatra; and the **MGM Grand's Theme Park** (opening February 1994) will have some wild rides. And no one of any age should miss the show-stopping Volcanic eruption outside the **Mirage**.

LADIES OF THE NIGHT

This may come as news, but prostitution is illegal in Clark County, of which Las Vegas is very much a part. But just over the county line, well, that's another story. And within Vegas itself, you can certainly find your pick of strip clubs and other adult entertainment. In the newspaper boxes found all along the Strip and Downtown, you'll find no shortage of advertisements for companionship.

SPORTS AND RECREATION

Off the Strip, there's everything any prime vacation spot of comparable size can offer - miniature golf, city parks offering a full range of activities, fun and sun in the hotel swimming pool.

Some of the finest golf courses anywhere are in Las Vegas, which is why the LPGA and other leading tournaments come to town every year to hold their world-class contests. The **Desert Inn Hotel** has a superb course, as does the **Canyon Gate Country Club**, where the annual Sand Bash Open is held; altogether Las Vegas has 23 excellent courses in the area.

And since the weather is so good year round, you can also enjoy great tennis, swimming, hiking, boating, and just about anything else that comes to mind - including bungee jumping adjacent to Circus Circus. When the weather turns a bit cold and snowy up in the mountains west of town, you've got first-rate skiing and other snow-bound activities in **Mt. Charleston's Lee Canyon**.

EXCURSIONS

Within city limits, Vegas has some of the most unique and unusual places to visit, from the world famous **Liberace Museum**, where you can see Mr. Entertainment's furs, capes, tiled pianos, and pink Rolls Royces, to **Ripley's Believe It Or Not Odditorium**, where you can view a torture chamber, see shrunken heads, and gaze at a huge roulette wheel made entirely of jelly beans, to the **Imperial Palace Auto Collection**, housing a car-lovers' dream-come-true collection of more than 200 historical and fascinating cars.

Outside of town, first-rate attractions lie waiting for you, from the engineering marvel of nearby **Hoover Dam**, to boating, rafting, and swimming in **Lake Mead**, to the majesty of **Valley of Fire State Park**, to the helicopter flight-seeing vistas looking into the incomparable **Grand Canyon**.

DAYLIFE AND NIGHTLIFE

Now that you have some idea of the kinds of possibilities Las Vegas has to offer, we'd like to introduce you to the city's neighborhoods. For ease of reference we're dividing Vegas into the Strip, Downtown, and Greater Las Vegas. Each part of town has its own feel and style, but they're all still Vegas: fun, exciting, and alluring.

THE STRIP!

The fabled **Las Vegas Strip** may well be America's most famous street. It's a neon-filled, glitzy scene night after night, a street where big dreams are dreamt and fortunes made. Of course, you can lose here too, but that's all part of the thrill of taking a risk and trying to beat the odds. If you risk nothing, you win nothing - every time!

The Strip (Las Vegas Boulevard South), coined by a retired L.A. cop-turned-club owner, was named after Sunset Strip in Los Angeles. In years past, the Strip was defined as that part of Las Vegas Blvd. S. between the **Hacienda Hotel** on the southern end and the **Sahara Hotel** on the northern end, but today most people extend the Strip a few blocks further north to Bob Stupak's **Vegas World**.

The Strip is the heart and soul of Las Vegas, a three-mile long stretch of casinos, hotels, restaurants, and junk-filled souvenir shops. At night, you can't help getting caught up in the excitement of Vegas, even if you don't gamble. Just walking through one of the mega-resorts along the Strip can be a fun way to spend the night. You'll certainly get your fill of interesting people-watching.

You may notice that casinos don't have clocks on the wall, nor are there any windows in most places. The casinos want you to forget time and concentrate on the task at hand: gambling! You'll be offered free liquor, and sometimes free cigarettes. At many hotels, as we've indicated, the food is usually cheap, plentiful, and quite palatable. Buffet dining has been refined to a high art in Vegas, both on the Strip and Downtown.

The Strip continues to change, with new hotel and casino additions and subtractions. The venerable **Dunes Hotel and Casino**, long a landmark on the Strip next door to **Caesars Palace**, recently closed and was purchased by veteran hotel builder **Steve Wynn** of **Mirage/Treasure Island/Golden Nugget** fame. As of this writing, all we know is that the Dunes will come down and something new will go up in its place. The first Strip hotel and casino, the **El Rancho,** has also closed after many years of operation, as has the **Paddlewheel** just off the Strip.

As long as you're not cruising from one end of the Strip to the other, most casinos are within easy walking distance, and you won't need transportation.

DOWNTOWN

The old expression, "Not all that glitters is gold," may not be much used in this corner of Nevada, but visitors should keep this useful saying in mind as they wander through the maze of neon in Downtown Vegas known as **Glitter Gulch**. This is where modern Las Vegas began, where gambling really took off.

While Downtown is smaller than the Strip, and some-what more laid back (if such a thing is possible inVegas), there is more than enough to do in this compact area. During the day, Downtown looks a bit run down, but when night falls, with the neon blazing, the hawkers hawking, and the pedestrians gawking, Glitter Gulch takes on a whole new character. Downtown comes alive like few other places on Earth!

Downtown Las Vegas is bounded by the intersection of Las Vegas Boulevard and Fremont Street on the east, Bridger Avenue on the south, Main Street on the east, and Stewart Avenue on the north. Even though many folks call the whole area Glitter Gulch, the Gulch really is a small area on and around Fremont Street. **Vegas Vic** and **Sassy Sally**, the neon cowboy and cowgirl dating from the halcyon days of the 1950's, welcome you to Downtown's hotels and casinos from their respective perches on opposite sides of Fremont Street.

You won't find nearly as many big production shows, huge casinos, or recreational choices as the Strip, so bear this in mind when you're deciding where to stay. But we'll wager you'll have big fun and a great time in either place!

GREATER LAS VEGAS

There's a whole lot of Vegas out there beyond the Strip and Downtown worth exploring. The most popular tourist attraction, the **Liberace Museum**, is well off the Strip, not far from the airport. You've got a big selection of attractions here, from the **Southern Nevada Zoo** to the **Las Vegas Art Museum** (one of the best art museums in the country) to **Ethel M Chocolates** to see how the Mars products are made. And, of course, outside city limits you've got **Hoover Dam**, **Lake Mead**, **Mt. Charleston**, and **Valley of Fire State Park**, to name just a few.

Greater Las Vegas is where most residents live. In order to see it, you'll need some kind of transportation to get there, whichever "there" you happen to be heading to. We include places well east or west of the Strip, not to mention north of Downtown and way south.

If you don't want 24-hour a day non-stop glitter and excitement - if you want to slow down a bit - you should think about staying outside the Strip or Downtown. We wouldn't recommend this for convention delegates or people visiting for the first time, but repeat visitors who know they want a less crazy pace may find the greater Las Vegas metropolitan area just what the doctor ordered.

CURRENT HAPPENINGS

When the current building spree is finished later this year and early next, including major additions at the Circus Circus **Luxor** resort, the **MGM Grand Hotel and Theme Park**, and Mirage's **Treasure Island**, there will be nearly 90,000 hotel rooms, far more per capita than any other sizable city.

Las Vegas today is a vibrant, expanding city, where a good time can be had for a relatively small amount of money. Whether you're moving to the area or are just visiting, there's plenty to do during the day and at night for folks of all ages.

Las Vegas is truly one of America's special cities; we've done our best to bring you the best it has to offer and are confident your'll have a great time. Read on!

THE BEST OF LAS VEGAS

Best Buffet:	*Mirage, Bally's*
Best Steak:	*William B's (Stardust); The Steak House (Circus Circus)*
Best Pizza:	*California Pizza Kitchen*
Best Shrimp Cocktail:	*Golden Gate Hotel (for 99¢)*
Best Outdoor Activity:	*Wet 'n Wild Water Park*
Best Dancing:	*Palladium (Country & Western); Shark Club (rock)*
Best Dam:	*Hoover Dam (okay, so we're having some fun here)*
Best Production Show:	*Splash (Riviera); Folies Bergere (Tropicana)*
Best Magic Show:	*Siegfried and Roy*
Best Excursion:	*Red Rock Canyon*
Best Shopping:	*Caesars Forum*
Best Special Cinema:	*Magic MotionMachines (Excalibur); Omnimax Theater (Caesars Palace)*
Best Free Concerts:	*Jaycee Park*
Best Special Effect:	*Volcano erupting in front of The Mirage*
Best Egyptian Pyramid:	*Luxor*
Best Romantic Spot:	*Mount Charleston Lodge, northwest of town*
Best Guidebook:	**Las Vegas Guide** *(Passport Press) - of course!*

3. LAS VEGAS HISTORY

EARLY BEGINNINGS

The first whispers of modern day Las Vegas (Spanish for **The Meadows**) can be traced back to the late 1820s, perhaps even 1830, the year that traders found a shortcut en route from New Mexico to Los Angeles along the Spanish Trail, and became the first non-Indians to set foot in the area later to be known as Las Vegas. This new shortcut through Paiute Indian territory eventually doomed the Paiute, as more and more traders, and then Mormon missionaries, used the route for moving their goods and religious wares.

An ill-fated attempt to colonize Las Vegas Valley failed in the early 1850's, as an attempt by Mormon missionaries to establish a mission, initially successful, fell into disarray as crop failures worsened tensions among and between the missionaries and miners, and finally caused the entire settlement to disband.

LT. JOHN FREMONT

*Southern Nevada was first mapped by the U.S. military. Army cartographer **John Fremont** was assigned the task, and after two trips had produced maps of the entire region. On his first visit, he camped around what is today Las Vegas Springs outside town. He was rewarded with his perseverance and outdoor skills years after his death by having streets and hotels named after him. Pretty cool being an explorer, huh?*

THE RAILROAD

As in so many other places in the Wild West, it was the advent of the mighty railroad that established Las Vegas and put it on the map. Chosen as a crossroads in the late 1800s due to its plentiful water supply and, of course, strategic location, a railroad town soon sprung up, and Las Vegas was off and running.

A few years later, in 1905, the town became a city when the San Pedro, Los Angeles, and Salt Lake Railroad (later to become the Union Pacific Railroad) made it a hub of sorts - a railroad division point.

GAMBLING COMES TO TOWN

1931 was the seminal year in the history of Las Vegas. That year the Hoover Dam began construction and Governor Fred Balzar legalized gambling. A separate bill in 1931 also influenced events to come: it allowed a divorce to become legal and binding after just six weeks, the nation's first quickie divorce law.

This came into play immediately, when Hollywood movie moguls and screen stars began making the divorce pilgrimage, first to Reno, and then, with the completion of the Hoover Dam in 1935 (bringing in its wake new hotels and casinos), to Las Vegas.

Gambling did not really take off in Vegas for quite a few years, largely because conservative Mormons controlled the politics and much of the business of the city. The first hotel/casino on the Strip opened in 1941, the **El Rancho Vegas**. The innovative El Rancho was a big hit, and showed other developers the tremendous potential of combining a casino with a hotel and a showroom.

With the opening of mobster Benjamin "Bugsy" Siegel's **Flamingo Hotel** in 1946, Las Vegas replaced Reno as the

king of Nevada's gambling cities, a title it never relin-
quished. Bugsy's big, glitzy casino, the first of its kind in
Vegas, was the first to attract the high-rollers. They now had
a luxurious place where they could spend their money in
style. There was now bait to attract the *whales*, the term
used in today's casino parlance for the highest of the high-
rollers. Las Vegas had come of age.

The city prospered, but its reputation as a gangster
hangout and center of prostitution grew too. The association in the public's eye of mobsters with Las Vegas held back
the city's growth. In fact, Las Vegas was often referred to
in this period as **Sin City**.

HOWARD HUGHES

This was a time of especially colorful characters, people
like **Nick the Greek**, one of the most famous gamblers in
Vegas; the **Binion family**, owners of the famous Binion
Horseshoe Casino; and **Howard Hughes**, the iconoclastic
and secretive billionaire who arrived on the scene in 1967
and lent Las Vegas the legitimacy it had long been seeking.
Vegas was seen in a new light and began a remarkable
period of growth that continues to this day.

Rumor has it that Hughes moved to the Desert Inn, one
of the ritziest hotels on the Strip, rented out all the rooms
on the top floor, and decided to stay for a while. Hughes
did not gamble. The owner, Cleveland crime boss Moe
Dalitz, wanted Hughes out so he could move some whales
into his best suites, but Hughes enjoyed the creature
comforts and was not interested in moving. So, the story
goes, he bought the hotel for $13 million.

Hughes then went on a buying spree that ended with
him owning a good portion of Las Vegas, including six
hotel/casinos, lots of land, the local airport, and practically

everything else not nailed down to the desert floor.

Today's casino moguls are men like **Bill Harrah** (of Harrah's hotel chain fame), **Kirk Kerkorian** (master real-estate developer and owner of the MGM hotel), and **Steve Wynn** (CEO of Mirage Enterprises) - but Howard Hughes, Old Spruce Goose himself, the man who changed the face of Vegas, occupies the highest rung on the grandiose ladder of Las Vegas myth-making.

LAS VEGAS TODAY

Fed by one of the healthiest tourist trades in the country, Las Vegas is growing faster than any other major city in America, and has been for a long time. This growth is fueled at least in part by the absence of state income and corporate taxes, and of course by gambling and gambling-related revenues.

The current population of **Clark County** stands at 875,000, with just under half living in Las Vegas proper (but the suburbs that have sprawled out from Vegas city limits are for all intents and purposes part of the city). At the current rate of influx, the population should easily surpass one million before the end of 1995.

Tourism is so healthy, in fact, that last year there were a record 22 million visitors, and more are expected each year for the rest of this decade. And the crowd is getting younger.

The federal government employs quite a few locals. More than 12,000 people work at **Nellis Air Force Base** and the **Nevada Test Site**, with tens of thousands more indirectly employed. The future of both military facilities is up in the air owing to a shrinking military force and the possibility of eliminating all nuclear weapons tests after 1996. **The University of Nevada at Las Vegas (UNLV),** founded in 1963, is also a significant employer.

Supposedly, Vegas is now mostly devoid of organized crime. The casinos are legitimate big business, tightly regulated by the **Nevada Gaming Commission** and the **Nevada Control Board**. The FBI keeps a close watch as well. Whether the mob still has a hand in the gambling industry, and just what it is they still control, remains the subject of controversy and debate inside and outside of town. Regardless, gambling is a big business in Vegas - $4 billion in gambling revenues in 1992.

While the official gambling take has not yet been published, it looks like 1993 was another hugely successful year for the gambling mecca known as Las Vegas. This amazing and exciting city has come a long way from its sleepy origins as a railroad town. *The Meadows* no longer, Las Vegas has truly come into its own.

LAS VEGAS CITY MAP

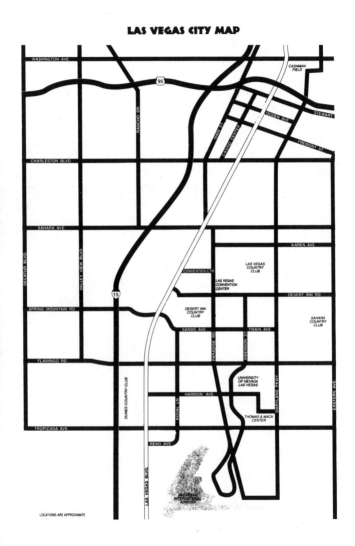

4. BASIC INFORMATION

Las Vegas is an easy town to get around. Most of the big hotels on the Strip are within walking distance from each other, as are the casinos in the smaller Downtown area, though you'll need transportation between the two or to get to most area excursions. You can leave your worries behind: the Downtown and Strip casino areas are safe to walk, day or night, as long as you stick to the beaten path.

ORIENTATION

Las Vegas sits at the southeastern tip of the state of Nevada, near the confluence of three states: California to the west, Utah to the northeast, and Arizona to the east and southeast. Situated in a beautiful valley about 2,100 feet above sea level, Las Vegas has fairly low humidity, 29 percent on average, but is pretty hot most of the year.

All of Nevada lies in the Pacific Standard Time zone, and the state observes Daylight Savings Time.

ARRIVALS AND DEPARTURES

By Air

The point of entry and exit for 22 million visitors in Las Vegas is the large and modern **McCarran International Airport** (general information number: 702/261-5743; terminal paging: 702/261-5733).

Nineteen airlines serve Las Vegas, as do many charter services. Charter flights are way up, and McCarran's addition of eight gates in their new charter terminal makes Vegas' airport one of the nicest, most modern facilities in the nation. There are moving escalators to help you with the long distances between gates.

The airport is spotlessly clean, and you can indulge your gambling appetite right off the plane. Slot machines are ringing, clanging, banging, and bojangling everywhere.

When departing Vegas by air, don't cut your time too short. Getting to your destination gate can be an interminably long distance, and if you don't leave yourself enough time, you're going to feel like O.J. Simpson in the Hertz commercial - running long and hard with your luggage trying to catch that plane. We know - we've done it all too often!

So you can do some comparison shopping for fares, we've listed all the airlines that fly to and from Las Vegas. The easiest way to go, of course, is to pick up a phone and call your travel agent, and let him or her take care of it.

But if you want to call yourself, we've listed the airlines that service Vegas (listing the 800 toll-free number only for those airlines that have them).

If you want to know the weather prior to your arrival, call the **National Weather Service Recording for Las Vegas and Vicinity** at 702/734-2010.

AIRLINES
- **Air Nevada** (702/736-8900)
- **Air Canada** (800-776-3000)
- **America West** (800/247-5692)
- **American** (800/433-7300)
- **American Trans Air** (800/225-9920)
- **Continental** (800/525-0280)
- **Delta** (800/221-1212)
- **Golden Pacific** (800/352-3281)
- **Hawaiian Air** (800/2277110)
- **Northwest** (800/225-2525)
- **Scenic Airlines** (702/739-1900)
- **SkyWest** (800/453-9417)
- **Southwest** (800/531-5601)
- **Sun Country Airlines** (800/359-5786)
- **StatesWest** (800/247-3866)
- **Taesa** (800/328-2372)
- **TWA** (800/221-2000)
- **United** (800/241-6522)
- **USAir** (800/772-4368)

FROM THE AIRPORT TO THE CITY

Limos and Taxis
The city's bus service (Citizens Area Transit) does not run out to the airport, but McCarran is close in, just one mile south of the Strip and about five miles from Downtown. You might want to consider taking one of the three main limousine services in front of the terminal ($4.00 to the Strip or $5.50 to Downtown).

The limo services are also available for chauffeuring you around town during your stay, but it'll cost you more than the ride from the airport. The **Gray Line** airport shuttle is the same price, but not as much fun as a limo.

The limos are:
· **Bell Transportation** (702/736-4428)
· **Lucky 7** (702/739-6177)
· **Presidential** (702/731-5577)

Taxis are also readily available at the terminal, but it'll cost you about twice as much: $7-10 to the Strip; $10-15 to Downtown.

Check with your hotel before you arrive to see if they offer free limo or van pickup from the airport.

CAR RENTALS

If you want to rent a car, a number of car rental agencies have cars waiting for you just outside the airport (shuttle buses pick you up on the street across from the baggage claim area) and at selected hotels in the city. It's always a good idea to call ahead and book a car, especially during the peak tourist season in April and May.

Following are just a few of the many car rental agencies:
· **Avis** (800/331-1212)
· **Alamo** (800/327-9633)

- **Hertz** (800/654-3131)
- **Ajax** (702/477-0277)
- **Alamo** (702/737-3111)
- **Avon Rent A Car** (702/386-6717)
- **Brooks Rent-a-Car** (702/735-3344)
- **Budget** (702/736-1212)
- **Dollar Car Rental** (702/739-8408)
- **Payless Car Rental** (702/739-8488)
- **Thrifty Car Rental** (702/736-8227)
- **Valley Rent A Car** (702/732-8282)

BY BUS

Greyhound buses serve Las Vegas from all directions. The bus lets you off Downtown at 200 S. Main St. near Jackie Gaughan's Plaza Hotel (formerly the Union Plaza Hotel). It is the cheapest way to travel by far. The phone number for the bus station is 702/384-9561 or 800/231-2222.

BY CAR

If you're coming by car, make sure you have a full tank of gas, a spare tire, and plenty of water. Gas stations are few and far between on some stretches of the road, and you wouldn't want to get caught short in the middle. Even if your car is in great shape, bring plenty of water as emergency protection against overheating. It's a hot desert out there.

Driving long distances in the glaring sun can wear your eyes out fast, so don't forget a good pair of sunglasses for long daytime hauls. And we certainly hope your air conditioning is working. As we said above, temperatures climb into the 100's, and you might soon get to know what dough goes through to become bread.

Driving conditions are generally good, but you should

be aware that there are occasional sandstorms and winter snowstorms in the high passes, and there could be the inevitable road paving and construction delays.

Here are two numbers you might want to call:

· For **Nevada road conditions** within Nevada, call 702/ 486-3116

· For **California road conditions**, call the **CHP - California Highway Patrol** at 213/736-3374.

DIRECTIONS

· **From LA**, take any major highway to I-10 heading west (the San Bernadino Freeway), past Ontario, and take I-15 north all the way into town. The trip is about 290 miles and should take about 4 1/2 hours. It's 55 mph till you hit I-15, then 65 mph all the way home. In the good old days, before the speed limit was imposed in Nevada, drivers would race across the desert at speeds in excess of 100 mph, doing the open road, kicking up dust, and living the American dream.

There's sometimes heavy fog near the Angeles Forest, and in the winter the passes in the high desert above 4000 feet may get snowed in and require chains or even be closed altogether. Most of the trip is in California (only 41 miles are in Nevada), so you might also want to listen to radio stations such as KNX for local weather conditions, or call the CHP for updates.

· From other points in **Southern California** you'll still want to hook up with **I-15** and take it all the way into town as discussed above.

· From **Northeastern Nevada**, take **Route 93** until you hit **I-15,** and go south.

· From **Utah**, take **I-15** south until you see the neon.

· From **Northwestern Nevada**, take **Route 95** south straight

into Las Vegas.
- From **Phoenix or Tucson**, go north on **Route 93** (you'll pass **Lake Mead National Recreation Area**).
- From the **east** (and if your route takes you past Flagstaff, Arizona, just south of the **Grand Canyon**), take **Interstate 40** which becomes **Route 93.**

A COUPLE OF QUICK TIPS

- *Don't bet more than you can afford to lose.*
- *Big conventions bring in a ton of people, especially the annual **Comdex Convention** (November) and the **Consumer Electronics Show** (January). You should make reservations in advance during these conventions because it's extremely difficult to get rooms during these two shows.*
- *The spring and fall are the busy seasons. It's usually possible to get a room somewhere - after all, there are currently in excess of 76,000 rooms with nearly another 10,500 in the works - but to get a room in your desired hotel you may want to book in advance.*
- *Remember, Las Vegas is in the desert. It gets really hot, so it's a good idea to drink plenty of fluids.*
- *Traffic: it's the pits. Long lights, especially on the Strip, will definitely slow you down, particularly in the evenings. Take Industrial Road behind the Strip whenever possible.*
- *Book the big production shows in advance. The bigger ones often get sold out early.*
- *We'll say it again: don't bet more than you can afford to lose. Know your limit and stick to it. Take the money management advice in our **Casino Basics and Money-Management** chapter seriously.*

BY TRAIN

Amtrak (800/872-7245) will take you right into Las Vegas's Union Station in Downtown Vegas, where, as at the airport, you can start gambling immediately inside the train station. The train station is adjacent to Jackie Gaughan's Plaza Hotel. Unless you're taking a cross-country train from the East or Midwest, you'll likely end up on the *Desert Wind*, which is the L.A.-Las Vegas-Salt Lake City run. From LA, the City of Angels, travel time by train is seven hours; from Salt Lake, about nine hours.

GETTING AROUND TOWN

By Foot

It's easy to walk the Strip or Downtown. You won't need transportation within these areas unless you're at a hotel away from the Strip's center, are feeling a but lazy, or get withered by a hot desert sun that goes as high as 115 degrees in the summer.

However, if you're going from the Strip to Downtown, you'll probably need transportation as the distance is about four miles. All other areas require transportation to get around, be it by car, bus, taxi, limo or divine movement.

By Car

If you're not going to walk, you'll want to cruise by car. The street grid is easy to follow, and most things of a tourist nature within city limits are fairly close in. If you need to rent a car, see the list of agencies on pages 30-31.

If you're planning to visit places like Hoover Dam, Lake Mead, or Valley of Fire State Park, you've got more flexibility if you drive there yourself than going on a tour, where your time is not your own.

By Bus

Buses are an easy and cheap way to get around town. **Las Vegas Area Transit** (702/384-3540) runs the **Citizens Area Transit**, or **CAT** (702/228-7433), which administers the city's bus system. The buses are frankly not as fast as the schedule says, but on the whole they're fairly reliable. Most of you will use the two main routes for the Strip and Downtown, but the system also extends well out into the greater Las Vegas metropolitan area. Call CAT for fare and schedule information for all routes.

The **Strip Bus** (sometimes called the **Strip Shuttle**) operates up and down the Strip, as the name implies, between the Hacienda and the Desert Inn hotels on Las Vegas Blvd. S., and over to the Hilton Hotel on Convention Center Drive. During the week, the Shuttle buses start their runs at 8:30 am and continue to 1:00 am, and are scheduled to depart every 15 minutes. The fare is $1.10 and **exact change is required**. You can get a discount commuter card good for 10 rides.

The Downtown bus - the **Glitter Gulch** - leaves from the **Downtown Transportation Center**, corner of Stewart and Casino Center Blvd. one block from the Lady Luck Hotel every 15 minutes from 7:00 am to 12:45 am and less frequently (you may need to wait as long as an hour) between 12:45 am and 7:00 am.

By Trolley

There are two trolley services to choose from, depending on where you are. The privately-owned and operated **Las Vegas Strip Trolley** (702/382-1404) covers the same route as the **Strip Shuttle** bus, with the added feature of dropping you off at the doorstep of most major hotels. The charge is $1.00 (exact change required as with the buses).

The Strip Trolley runs until 2:00 am, but takes longer than the bus to get from point A to point B.

The **Downtown Trolley** (702/799-6024) is a bargain at 50 cents. The trolley covers most of Downtown and is run by the city. The system closes down at 10:00 pm.

PARKING

Parking is not a problem as long as you pull up in front of virtually any hotel and leave your car with a valet (tip a dollar or two), or pull into the hotel's self-parking garage or lot. Parking is usually adjacent to the hotel and requires a short walk. For a one-spot or two-spot tip, valet parking is easy and certainly cheap.

TRAFFIC

A cautionary note about traffic in Las Vegas: it gets congested during morning and evening rush hour and on weekends, particularly along the Strip. The solution: take one of the alternative routes parallel to the Strip whenever heavy traffic looms, and use the back entrance to Strip hotels along Industrial Rd. On the east side of the Strip, use Paradise Road.

GUIDED BUS TOURS

There are three main guided bus tour companies you might want to consider, offering both city tours and tours to Hoover Dam, Lake Mead, the Grand Canyon, and other hot spots outside of town. The tour bus companies listed below also offer excursion trips. For more information about excursions, see our chapter on *Excursions and Day Trips*.

There are a number of reliable tour operators for city tours. The three biggies are:

- **Gray Line Tours**, 1550 S. Industrial Rd. (702/384-1234; 800/634-6579). Gray Line offers brief two hour tours and longer half-day tours. You will be picked up and deposited back at your hotel. Tours should cost about $25-30.
- **Ray and Ross**, 300 W. Owens Ave. (702/646-4661) offers half-day tours around town; evening night-clubbing tours beginning at 6 pm ($63); and dance tours beginning at 9:30 am ($38).
- **Guaranteed Tours**, 3734 Las Vegas Blvd. S. (702/369-1000) offers similar day and night city tours.

TAXIS

Cabs are plentiful (more than 600 citywide) and easy to hail on the Strip and Downtown, but a bit tougher outside the main tourist paths. They're lined up at virtually every hotel and can usually be hailed as they ply the main roads looking for a fare. If you're dining out, the restaurant can call for you as well.

The rates recently went up 50¢; it'll now cost you $2.20 to climb in and then $1.40 for every mile thereafter, with nominal extra charges for more than three passengers. If you do need to call a cab, here are some of the main taxi companies:

- **Yellow and Checker Cab** (702/873-2227)
- **Desert Cab** (702/736-1702)
- **Whittlesea Blue Cab** (702/384-6111)
- **ABC** (702/736-8444)
- **Ace** (702/736-8383)
- **Star** (702/873-2000).

LIMOUSINES

If taking a cab is not your bag, go for a limo. They're

a fun way to travel in style, if you can afford it or simply want to splurge. The rates are reasonable compared to some cities - a range of $22 an hour to $120 an hour for one particular huge stretch limo (the Longride Limousine, mentioned below).

The standard limo offers a comfortable ride and a few amenities, like stereo sound and a car phone. The stretch limos (about $10-20 more than the cost of a regular limo) include bar service, cellular phone, color TV, stereo, and other amenities.

Call one of the following limo services:
· **Bell Transportation** (702/736-4428, or 702/385-5466)
· **Lucky 7** (702/739-6177)
· **Presidential** (702/731-5577).

For the monster stretch limo, which includes a hot tub and a bartender, among other luxuries, call **Longride Limousine** (702/735-5211). If you have a group of ten or so, this might be more affordable than the $120 fee sounds. What the heck, you're in Vegas - why not?

FUN BOOKS

Fun books are free coupons given out in most hotels and casinos. You can pick them up in the lobby of most hotels, or just ask one of the receptionists or employees in your hotel. You can also usually find them in the complementary tourist magazines like **What's On in Las Vegas** or **Today in Las Vegas**. The coupons offer things like free drinks, gambling incentives such as three-for-two dollar plays at the tables, free pulls at slots, discounts on meals, and the like.

BANKING

Now that you've spent all that money shopping (not to mention gambling), you'll need to replenish your cash stockpile. Most banks are open from 9:00 am - 5:00 pm Monday through Thursday, 9:00 am - 5:30 pm Friday, and 10:00 am - 1:00 pm on Saturday. The **Las Vegas Chamber of Commerce** (2301 E. Sahara Ave.; 702/457-4664) can provide more details of other financial services.

You should have no trouble using traveler's checks in casinos to buy chips. If you have good credit, you may be able to take out a line of credit at most casinos, but call first and make sure that you can provide them with the necessary documentation (usually something like credit cards or a driver's license; some may require a bank statement).

Many casinos now have automatic teller machines (ATM's), where you should be able to use either your local ATM card if it's part of a larger network, or your VISA, Mastercard, or other major credit card. Watch out, though: a number of hotel ATM machines charge you a fee for using the service beyond the normal token charge you'd find elsewhere.

CLIMATE

Las Vegas Valley sits in the middle of the desert, actually the confluence of three deserts: **the Mojave, Sonoran,** and the **Great Basin**. As you might guess, then, the temperature here can get pretty hot. The city is surrounded by mountains, the highest peak of which is **Mt. Charleston** west of the city at just under 12,000 feet. There is very little rainfall - about 4.2 inches a year, and an average of 294 days of sunshine, including partially sunny days. It is dry, windy, and hot most of the time.

July and August are the hottest months, when the daily

maximum temperature can top 100 degrees. Be prepared: dress lightly and wear a hat. It also rains more at this time of the year, but bear in mind that annual rainfall is just over 4 inches a year.

January and December are the coolest months; the average maximum is 60 degrees, but it can go below freezing so bring at least one warm jacket or sweater if you're planning to visit anytime in the winter. The spring and autumn months are the most temperate, with average temperatures in the 70's and 80's.

If you want Vegas all to yourself, come during the last two weeks of December.

You can wear just about anything you want to in Las Vegas, although some of the fancier restaurants and shows may prefer formal dress. But casual dress for almost anything is the rule.

AVERAGE DAILY MAXIMUM AND MIMIMUM		
• January	54	34
• February	59	35
• March	66	42
• April	81	54
• May	90	63
• June	102	72
• July	105	78
• August	104	75
• September	87	62
• October	80	54
• November	62	40
• December	60	36

HEALTH SERVICES

Las Vegas has six main hospitals, most offering a full range of medical services. Two of them have 24-hour emergency rooms:

- **University Medical Center**, 1800 W. Charleston Blvd. (702/383-2000).
- **Humana Hospital Sunrise**, further out at 3186 Maryland Pkwy (702/731-8000).

Other area hospitals include:

- **Community Hospital**, 1409 E. Lake Mead Blvd., North Las Vegas (702/649-7711).
- **Desert Springs Hospital**, 2075 E. Flamingo Rd. (702/733-8000).
- **Valley Hospital**, 620 Shadow Ln. (702/388-4000).
- **Womens Hospital**, 2025 E. Sahara Ave. (702/735-7106).

If you need a doctor or dentist for non-emergencies, call the **Clark County Medical Society** (702/739-9989) or the **Clark County Dental Society** (702/435-7767).

SERVICES FOR THE DISABLED

If you or someone you're traveling with is disabled, you might want to call ahead and find out what special services are available and where. Las Vegas is better than many other cities in adapting its buildings and services for the disabled.

Write or call one of the following agencies:

- **Nevada Association for the Handicapped** (6200 W. Oakey Blvd., Las Vegas, NV 89102 (702/870-7050).
- **Southern Nevada Sightless Society**, 1001 N. Bruce St., Las Vegas, NV 89101 (702/642-0100), offers help and advice for sightless travelers.

Both **Amtrak** (800/USA-RAIL) and **Greyhound** (800/531-5332) offer discounts and special assistance to those in need.

PLACES OF WORSHIP

Whether you simply want to pray for a lucky streak at the gaming tables or desire reflective moments alone, we've included some local houses of worship. According to local lore, Las Vegas has more churches and synagogues per capita than any other city in America - almost 500!

Even though the city was founded by Mormons and remains roughly one-quarter Mormon, there is only one Mormon temple, the relatively new **Las Vegas Nevada Temple of the Church of Jesus Christ of Latter-day Saints**, 827 Temple View Dr. (702/438-7488). Situated above the city, there is a pretty view of the Valley down below.

Here are some of the bigger and better-known houses of worship, should the urge hit you:

- **Guardian Angel Cathedral** at 302 E. Desert Inn Rd. (702/735-5241), a Catholic church that is the closest church to the Strip. The church draws big crowds, particularly for Saturday afternoon Mass.
- **St. Joan of Arc**, 315 S. Casino Center Blvd. (702/382-9909), Catholic.
- **First Baptist Church**, 300 S. 9th St. (702/382-6177).
- **First Southern Baptist Church**, 700 E. St. Louis Ave. (702/732-3100).
- **Reformation Lutheran**, 580 E. St. Louis Ave. (702/732-2052), the big Lutheran church in town.
- **First United Methodist**, 231 S. Third St. (702/382-9939), the main Methodist church.
- **Temple Beth Sholom**, 1600 E. Oakey Blvd. (702/384-5070), the main Jewish synagogue.

TIPS FOR SENIOR CITIZENS

Discounts for senior citizens are often available for the asking. Discounts abound on everything from airfare, hotels, restaurants, car rentals, national parks, area attractions and other items, so it pays to get some details from the right sources. Vegas is a great town for discounts, so seniors can usually do pretty well for themselves here.

You might want to join the **American Association of Retired Persons (AARP)** for a mere five-spot. Make sure you bring along the membership card that will prove you are indeed over fifty. Their address and phone number is 1990 K St., NW, Washington, DC 20049 (202/872-4700). Ask for the **AARP Travel Service**. The folks at the AARP Travel Service will be able to send you information about senior discounts for your Las Vegas vacation.

If you're over 62 and a U.S. citizen or permanent resident - and can prove it - you can get a **Golden Age Passport** at the entrance of any national park. You and others traveling in a private car may then enter for free henceforward. What a country!

Both **Amtrak** (800/USA-RAIL) and **Greyhound** (800/531-5332) offer discounts if you book in advance. Call for more details.

Whether you're seeking general information or specific activities and events for seniors, call or visit the **Senior Citizens Center of Las Vegas and Clark County** located Downtown at 450 E. Bonanza, four blocks from Casino Center Blvd. (702/229-6454).

If you're thinking of retiring in Las Vegas, and would like to live in a planned community with all the amenities, one option is **Del Webb's Sun City Las Vegas**. Situated eight miles outside of town in close proximity to the Spring Mountain Range, Sun City has an 18 hole golf course and a community center featuring all manner of sports and swimming. Call 702/363-5454 for more information.

> ## THINKING OF MOVING TO VEGAS?
> *Interested in moving to Las Vegas? The cost of living is slightly higher than the national average, but certain things are a pretty good deal, like utilities and food. The cost of health care is among the lowest in the western US. And you can't do better from a tax perspective: there's no state income tax, no personal income tax, no inheritance, gift or estate, franchise, inventory or corporate tax!*

TIPS FOR FOREIGN VISITORS

Our friends from abroad, especially those from just over the northern frontier, love Las Vegas like few other American cities. For many, the allure of Vegas is not just the prospect of a quick buck; for better or worse, many foreigners perceive Las Vegas as the quintessential American city.

Canada sends more of its citizens our way than any other country, with one million tourists to Las Vegas and Nevada. Trailing Canada by a comfortable margin are Great Britain, Germany, France, Spain, Brazil and Mexico. Japan is also sending more and more tourists, with many Japanese combining cheaper Nevada ski vacation packages with some gambling frenzy in Vegas and Reno.

If you need to change money, you'll get a better rate at most banks or foreign exchange shops than you will in the hotels and casinos. One exception to this is **American Foreign Exchange** in the Las Vegas Hilton (702/892-0100). You might also want to try **Foreign Money Exchange**, 3025 Las Vegas Blvd. S. (702/791-3301).

Passports and Visas

If you are visiting the US from abroad (other than Canada), you will need a **valid passport and visa**. There are limits on what you may bring in: $400 in duty-free gifts; one liter of alcohol (the booze will count against your $400 total); and 200 cigarettes or 100 cigars. You'll have to report on a customs form if you are carrying in more than $10,000 in US currency.

The US authorities are also touchy about bringing in agricultural produce and meat products, so if your plans call for importing some kind of foodstuff, do yourself a favor and contact the **US Customs Service** at 1301 Constitution Ave., NW, Washington, DC 20229 (202/566-8195).

It's a good idea to bring traveler's checks for the bulk of your cash, or even better, you can use most major credit cards at cash machines. But there has been a trend away from American Express cards since the vendor has to pay an additional processing charge that other cards do not require. You can exchange money at most hotels and banks, and of course at the airport.

Water and Electricity

The water in the United States is safe to drink, whether you get it from the tap in your hotel room or served to you in a restaurant. And you'll need plenty of it in Las Vegas, as it gets very steamy here when the sun hits its peak!

And since it's quite hot in Las Vegas, chances are that sooner or later you'll want to get around to shaving (your face or your legs, depending). If you fancy electric razors or electric Euro-toothbrushes, you'll probably need an adapter, since the current here is 110 volts.

TIPPING

This section applies to Americans as well, who often ask themselves the same question: how much should I tip this guy or doll? Tipping varies from country to country and continent to continent, so here a few rules for tipping

American-style. Of course, if you hit the million-dollar jackpot at Vegas World or Four Queens, you'll probably want to be more generous than the advice given here.

Unlike Europe, a gratuity is not built into the check at restaurants unless you have a party of more than a certain number, usually ten or more, although this varies from place to place. At the bar, leave a dollar for each round of drinks ordered. For good restaurant service, 15% is the norm. You can be a big tipper by leaving 20%, which many people leave if they feel the service was outstanding.

For taxis, the standard tip is 10%; 10-15% for limousines. Give your bellhop a dollar or two for bringing your bags to your room, $3 if you have a number of heavy bags; and leave anywhere from $7-10 a week for efficient maid service in your hotel room.

See the Casino Basics chapter for tipping at the tables.

MORE INFORMATION

Before you go, you might want to call or write the **Las Vegas Convention and Visitors Authority**, located at 3150 Paradise Rd., Las Vegas, NV 89109, or call 702/892-0711. The Convention and Visitors Authority can give you an up-to-the minute update on special events and show schedules for the time you'll be in Vegas.

Other useful folks to call, depending on your needs:

· **Las Vegas Chamber of Commerce**, 2301 E. Sahara, Las Vegas, NV 89104 (702/457-4664), who can fill you in on facts and figures about the area if you're interested in moving to town.

· **Nevada Commission on Tourism**, Capital Complex, Carson City, NV 89104 (800/638-2321), if you want more detailed information about things to do outside city limits or somewhere else in Nevada .

- **Las Vegas Events**, an events hotline of sorts (702/731-2115); find out by phone what's going on during your stay.

For those of you with more refined tastes, you might want to call two additional numbers for the arts beat:

- **Southern Nevada Arts Hotline**, any time of the day or night, at 702/385-4444, ext. 2172 to get an updated cultural calendar (art exhibits, symphony schedule, lectures).
- **UNLV Performing Arts Center** (702/739-3801) for the lowdown on what's shaking culturally at the University of Nevada at Las Vegas.

ESSENTIAL PHONE NUMBERS

No one likes to think about emergencies when the skies are blue and you're out on the open road, so we thought we'd take care of this kind of stuff for you.

For hospital emergencies, call:

- **Southern Nevada Memorial Hospital**, 1800 W. Charleston Blvd. (702/383-2000), or
- **Humana Hospital Sunrise**, further out at 3186 Maryland Pkwy (702/731-8000).
- **Phone number information** can be found by dialing **411**.
- **Emergency assistance** in the form of police, fire, or an ambulance can be obtained (hopefully speedily) by dialing **911**.
- **For non-emergency police help**, call 702/795-3111.
- If you run out of money and need to wire friends or relatives, go to or call the **Western Union** telegraph office at 517 Fremont St. (702/382-4322).

5. HOTELS AND CASINOS

Vegas is home to 12 of the 13 biggest mega-resort hotels in the world, including the soon-to-be-completed **MGM Grand Hotel and Theme Park**, opening in February 1994, which will be the largest resort hotel in the world at 5,009 rooms!

Many hotels and casinos have themes, like Aladdin's Arabian Nights or Excalibur's medieval Knights of the Round Table. And the best part of all is the pricing policy: with few exceptions, even the expensive hotels are not outrageous, because the hoteliers are more concerned with getting you into their casino than anything else.

That's why many hotels will usually comp their high-roller guests with free shows, dinners, and rooms. In fact, you don't have to be a high-roller to get *comped*. If you're a gambler, casinos figure they'll more than make up for the price of a room or a meal with your spending at the tables and slots.

We've ranked the hotels by cost, from Expensive to Moderate to Inexpensive, and arranged them geographically: the Strip (including those hotels near the Strip), Downtown, and Greater Las Vegas. But these categories don't always hold, since most hotels offer periodic specials. We've also recommended a few motels.

Let's start with the incomparable Strip!

COMPS, LAS VEGAS STYLE

*Comps, the Las Vegas gambling jargon for freebies, are readily available to the savvy gambler. Casinos will gladly supply you with comps for meals, shows, rooms, and even airfare. But it doesn't come free: you've got to earn it by showing the casinos enough **action**, or play, at the tables.*

What about your acquaintance who constantly gets comped for the whole deal - airfare, room, shows and food? Jealous? Don't be. These comps are earned the hard way, and in all likelihood, and believe me we know, these gamblers drop so much money at the tables that the casinos are glad to comp them the whole shebang - again and again. Wouldn't you?

If you're looking to earn comps by gambling, it will cost you far more than simply arranging your vacation as you normally would and gambling at your own pace. But if you're already a big player, comps are the way to go. The casinos will be more than happy to make you feel comfortable if you give them the chance at your gambling dollar.

How do you go about getting comps? It's simple - ask for them. The casino will let you know the deal. Or if you're already in the casino playing, don't be afraid to ask for some comps. A subtle suggestion to the pit boss such as, "How's the food in the grill?" or "How's the show?" should get the message across. If your play is seen as adequate, hey, have a good meal - on the house!

THE STRIP AND IMMEDIATE AREA MAP

1. Aladdin
2. Alexis Park
3. Algiers
4. Arizona Charlie's
5. Bally's
6. Barbary Coast
7. Boardwalk
8. Bourbon Street
9. Caesars Palace
10. Circus Circus
11. Continental
12. Debbie Reynolds
13. Desert Inn
14. Excalibur
15. Flamingo Hilton
16. Frontier
17. Gold Coast
18. Hacienda
19. Harrah's
20. Imperial Palace
21. Las Vegas Hilton
22. Luxor
23. Maxim
24. MGM Grand
25. Mirage
26. Palace Station
27. Rio
28. Riviera
29. Sahara
30. San Remo
31. Sands
32. Sheffield Inn
33. St. Tropez
34. Stardust
35. Treasure Island
36. Tropicana
37. Vegas World
38. Westward Ho

STRIP HOTELS AND CASINOS

Expensive

ALEXIS PARK

375 E. Harmon Ave., Las Vegas, NV 89109 (702/796-3300; 800/582-2228).

Rates: Expensive.

Amenities: 3 restaurants; coffee shop; bar/lounge; 2 tennis courts; 3 swimming pools; nine-hole putting green; health spa.

Features: the **Pegasus restaurant** is probably the best in town; wet bars in every room; some rooms with fireplaces.

Casino Action: none.

The Alexis Park Resort is one of the nicest hotels in town, and you'll pay through the teeth for all that niceness. Its claim to fame is that, unlike other prominent Las Vegas addresses, there is no casino here. If you don't mind shelling out the bucks, and you have no desire to gamble, stay here.

The hotel has a Mediterranean cast about it, with beautiful gardens, mini-waterfalls, and general opulence oozing out of every pore. The Alexis Park, located a few blocks from the Strip, has 500 suites, all very expensive.

BALLY'S CASINO RESORT

3645 Las Vegas Blvd. S., Las Vegas, NV 89109 (702/739-4111; 800/634-3434).

Rates: Expensive.

Amenities: 6 restaurants, including a great buffet; 2 swimming pools; 10 tennis courts (5 lit for night play); health spa; shopping; lounge; comedy club; big-name acts in 2 rooms.

Features: **Celebrity Room** features hot acts 6 nights a week; **Jubilee Theater** features *Jubilee!* show; **Bally Arcade** offers 40 glitzy, upscale shops; **Youth Center**; and wedding chapel.
Casino Action: baccarat; blackjack; craps; keno; roulette; slots; sports betting; video poker.

Bally's offers a huge casino and great entertainment. The buffet is top-flight, particularly their champagne brunch on Sunday. It's a huge place; there are 2,828 large, commodious, and brightly-decorated rooms and suites here. Bally's was formerly the MGM Grand, which burnt down in 1980 but is rising again: (Kirk Kerkorian, Bally's former owner and veteran casino magnate, is scheduled to open the 5,009 room **MGM Grand Hotel and Theme Park** in February 1994 a few blocks south.)

Bally's is an immense place, with plenty to do, from the nearly 1,000 slot machines and 84 blackjack tables, to the exclusive Bally Arcade shops, to tennis, working out, swimming, and more. Parents will love the Youth Center, with lots of of video games (non-gambling, of course!) and an ice cream parlor.

CAESARS PALACE
3570 Las Vegas Blvd. S., Las Vegas, NV 89109 (702/731-7110; 800/634-6001).
Rates: Expensive.
Amenities: plush rooms just like you always pictured; 8 restaurants and snack bars; 2 huge swimming pools; 8 tennis courts (2 lit); beautiful gardens and landscaping; luxurious health spa.
Features: statues and fountains galore; **Circus Maximus** showroom with name acts; **Caesars Forum** and **Appian Way** upscale shopping arcades; **Cleopatra's Barge** floating cocktail bar; the fantastic **Omnimax** movie theater; 3 (count

'em, 3!) casinos.

Casino Action: baccarat; blackjack; craps; keno; roulette; Pai Gow; poker; slots; sports betting; video poker.

Caesars Palace is everything you ever thought Vegas was, is, or should be. It's a huge place, done up in neo-Roman luxury. People-movers link you to all corners of Caesars vast empire. Many of the 1,518 rooms have mirrored walls and ceilings, and marble bathtubs with whirlpool jets. The most exclusive suites offer Jacuzzis, saunas and just about anything else you might want - and at $685 a clip they better! Caesar's Forum shopping arcade is the best in town.

Big world championship boxing matches are held here. While beginners are not discouraged from gambling here, be advised that Caesars Palace casinos are known for their high-rollers. You'll notice some gamblers at private tables, where big bets are being laid down. Good luck!

DESERT INN HOTEL AND CASINO

3145 Las Vegas Blvd. S., Las Vegas, NV 89109 (702/733-4444; 800/634-6906).

Rates: Expensive.

Amenities: 6 restaurants (including their big-time night-club); 1 very nice swimming pool; 18-hole golf course; 10 lit tennis courts; extensive health spa; big shopping arcade.

Features: Running Track and full-scale exercise equipment; whirlpool baths; name acts appear nightly in the **Crystal Room**; quality lounge acts.

Casino Action: baccarat; blackjack; craps; keno; roulette; slots; Pai Gow; poker; sports betting; video poker.

If you want to sound like an old Vegas insider, you can tell your cabbie that you're staying at the "DI." If you don't, we'll understand. One of the original Las Vegas hotels, the

Desert Inn is one of the best on the Strip, understated and elegant. This was Howard Hughes's hangout in the late 1960's. The golf course is justly famous and is the site of the annual LPGA tournament.

There are 821 rooms, all first-rate, most done in Southwestern style, of which 92 are suites. If you can afford it, some of the private suites come with your own swimming pool! Great health facilities here - they probably have the best set-up in town if you want to stay in shape for the endurance required to win big at the tables!

LAS VEGAS HILTON

3000 Paradise Rd., Las Vegas, NV 89109 (702/732-5111; 800/732-7117).
Rates: Expensive.
Amenities: 14 restaurants; health spa and sauna; large swimming pool; 6 tennis courts; shops.
Features: **Youth Hotel**; huge casino; gambling instruction on your TV; big showroom with big acts like **Wayne Newton**; lounge acts; putting green; shuffleboard; big convention business.
Casino Action: baccarat; blackjack; craps; keno; poker; roulette; slots; sports betting; video poker.

Set right next to the Las Vegas Convention Center, the enormous Hilton (formerly the International) has got a lot to offer, particularly in the food department with its wide array of generally good restaurants. This was Elvis Presley's only showroom in Las Vegas. It was also the site of the now-infamous Tailhook scandal of 1991.

The Hilton has 3,174 rooms, all of them spacious. Ask for a room in the 375-foot tower close to the top, if one is available; the view at night is just great. The Youth Hotel makes this place an excellent alternative to Circus Circus or

Excalibur; overnight lodging or hourly supervision are both available for children at very reasonable rates, with plenty of activities and sports. The casino is huge and attractive, with its sports betting area, the Superbook, the world's largest such facility.

THE MIRAGE

3400 Las Vegas Blvd. S., Las Vegas, NV 89109 (702/791-7111; 800/456-7111).

Rates: Expensive.

Amenities: 8 restaurants; 3 bars (including a sports bar); ice cream parlor; daycare/babysitting facilities; shopping arcade featuring exclusive stores; health spa; beauty salon; swimming pool/lagoons.

Features: the mock Volcano eruption every 30 minutes; **Siegfried and Roy**'s magic act, featuring white tigers, and other name acts in the **Theater Mirage**; an immense aquarium behind registration stocked with sharks and other dazzling aquatic life; dolphins out back.

Casino Action: baccarat; blackjack; craps; keno; Pai Gow; poker; roulette; slots; sports betting; video poker.

The Mirage is one of the finest resort hotels anywhere, a modern classic. When you make your way past the volcano (a must-see) and enter the front door, you're greeted by lush gardens, waterfalls, and tropical plants. The swimming pool is beautifully done, really several lagoons joined together. The restaurants are very good too. At a total cost of $630 million, we can't say whether owner Steve Wynn got his money's worth, but it sure is one hell of a show. Siegfried and Roy's magic and animal show is the most popular one in town, but at $75 admission it's quite an expense.

The Mirage is another of Las Vegas's growing mega-resorts serviced by thousands of employees. There are 3,049 rooms, with the more expensive rooms and suites done up in South Seas splendor. Parents will enjoy the convenient on-site daycare and the gambling, which goes on at all levels of expertise in the Mirage's beautiful Polynesian casino.

RIO SUITES HOTEL AND CASINO

3700 W. Flamingo, Las Vegas, NV 89109 (702/252-7777; 800/888-1808).

Rates: Expensive.

Amenities: 5 restaurants, (one of which is the international **"Carnival Buffet"**); 5 lounges with some name acts; swimming pool; health spa; shops.

Features: real-live white sand beach by the freshwater swimming pool.

Casino Action: blackjack; craps; Pai Gow; poker; slots; sports betting; video poker.

Not far from the Strip (at I-15 and Flamingo), the Rio lives up to its name through its Viva Brazil theme. You'll find a touch of Rio in each of the 424 rooms (all suites, hence the hefty price tag), not just in the lobby. Another 430 suites are under construction. Volleyball tournaments are commonplace at poolside on the only white sand beach you'll find in Vegas.

Moderate

ALADDIN HOTEL AND CASINO

3667 Las Vegas Blvd. S., Las Vegas, NV 89109 (702/736-0111; 800/634-3424).

Rates: Moderate.

Amenities: 5 restaurants; snack bar and coffee shop; 3

swimming pools; tennis courts; stores; beauty salon and barbershop.

Features: the 10,000 seat **Aladdin Theater**; nightly shows at the **Bagdad Showroom**.

Casino Action: baccarat; blackjack; craps; keno; poker Pai Gow Poker; roulette; slots; sports betting.

Despite a troubled past, the Aladdin seems to be back in the pink. Trivia buffs and Elvis aficionados will note that the King and his blushing bride were married here in 1967. The Aladdin has 1,100 rooms and is centrally located along the Strip.

DEBBIE REYNOLDS HOLLYWOOD HOTEL AND MOVIE MUSEUM

305 Convention Center Dr., Las Vegas, NV 89109 (702/734-0711)

Rates: Moderate.

Amenities: 2 restaurants; swimming pool.

Features: Movie Museum.

Casino Action: slots; video blackjack; video keno; video poker.

Debbie Reynolds has just arrived in town, with her brand spanking new Hollywood Hotel and Movie Museum. Located on the site of the old Paddlewheel Hotel, just up the block from the Convention Center, Debbie's place has been refurbished in true, glitzy Vegas style. The hotel has 200 rooms. Debbie will be appearing nightly herself in the Showroom, followed by a later show with comedian Rip Taylor. The museum will open in late 1993, featuring a large collection of Hollywood memorabilia (costumes, props, film clips) from the old movies.

EXCALIBUR

3850 Las Vegas Blvd. S., Las Vegas, NV 89109 (702/597-7777; 800/937-7777).

Rates: Moderate.

Amenities: 10 restaurants, most with medieval themes, except **Wild Bill's**, an Old West restaurant for you cowboys out there; 2 swimming pools; shops; miniature golf.

Features: built to resemble a medieval castle; **King Arthur's Arena** features 2 nightly dinner shows about King Arthur, complete with horses, jousts and sword-play; **Renaissance Village** and carnival games; **Magic Motion Machines**, an incredible combination movie/simulated ride; wedding chapel; 2nd-largest casino in town (100,000 square feet).

Casino Action: blackjack; craps; keno; poker; roulette; slots; sports betting; video poker.

Owned by Circus Circus Enterprises, Excalibur is one of the most exciting and fun *family* places on the Strip: it looks like every child's fantasy of ye olde medieval castle. It's a classic Vegas recreation of suspended reality, replete with knights in shining armor, damsels in distress (those losing at the tables, anyway), and gallant attendants dressed in their best Disney-esque Sherwood Forest garb. Again, bear in mind that the focus here is family; there are lots of kids running around!

The 4,032 rooms make Excalibur not just the biggest resort in town, but the biggest in the world (until Kirk Kerkorian's MGM Grand opens in February 1994 with 5,009 rooms)! The rooms are big enough and are supposed to be reminiscent of the days of yore, with the walls plastered with a "castle brick" motif. Excalibur offers a full range of games in their large but crowded casino.

FLAMINGO HILTON

3555 Las Vegas Blvd. S., Las Vegas, NV 89109 (702/733-3111; 800/732-2111).

Rates: Moderate.

Amenities: 10 restaurants, including nightly dinner show (except Sundays); 4 lit tennis courts; 2 swimming pools and Jacuzzi; video arcade; health spa; shops.

Features: Ice Skating dinner show.

Casino Action: baccarat; Big Six Wheel; blackjack; craps; keno; Pai Gow; poker; slots; sports betting; video poker.

The Flamingo was the first modern-era, big glitz hotel/casino in Las Vegas, opened by the infamous Bugsy Siegel in December 1946. The pink neon flamingos out in front welcome you to what is now just one of many huge Vegas extravaganzas.

Boasting 3,530 tastefully-decorated rooms (another 419 rooms are being added), the Flamingo has several good, inexpensive buffets, an excellent pool and a good variety of casino games. The Pot-O-Gold Jackpot in the slots arcade is a big attraction with its $1 million prize for the lucky gambler.

FRONTIER HOTEL

3120 Las Vegas Blvd. S., Las Vegas, NV 89109 (702/794-8200; 800/634-6966).

Rates: Moderate.

Amenities: 3 restaurants, 1 coffee shop; 1 swimming pool; 2 lit tennis courts; shops.

Features: No entertainment; in-house TV gambling instruction program; golf privileges at the Desert Inn; putting green; showroom.

Casino Action: baccarat; blackjack; craps; poker; slots; sports betting; video poker.

The Frontier is one of the older institutions along the Strip. Recently expanded, the hotel now has 986 rooms, most at reasonable rates. The place still has an Old West feel to it. At 100,000 square feet, Frontier's casino is one of the biggest around.

HACIENDA RESORT HOTEL AND CASINO
3950 Las Vegas Blvd. S., Las Vegas, NV 89119 (702/739-8911; 800/634-6713).
Rates: Moderate.
Amenities: 3 restaurants, including a buffet; 2 swimming pools; 6 lit tennis courts; shops; big showroom; lounge acts.
Features: Ice skating shows nightly; RV park out back.
Casino Action: blackjack; craps; roulette; slots; video poker.
The Hacienda marks the southernmost edge of the Strip, and is one of the city's older hotels. There are now 840 rooms, spare but nice, with a Southwestern motif throughout. The casino is not all that extensive, but the play is still good here.

HARRAH'S LAS VEGAS
3475 Las Vegas Blvd. S., Las Vegas, NV 89109 (702/369-5000; 800/634-6765).
Rates: Moderate.
Amenities: 5 restaurants, including a deli and an all-you-can-eat buffet; swimming pool; health spa; 4 bars and lounges; video arcade; shops; babysitting.
Features: good-sized theater featuring **"Spellbound,"** a magic show; hotel is designed like an old-time riverboat; good location on the Strip; Fun Book.
Casino Action: baccarat; bingo; blackjack; craps; keno; poker; roulette; slots; sports betting; video poker.
Formerly the Holiday Inn, it's now the biggest Harrah's

hotel with 1,725 modern rooms. Harrah's gets the highest score of any place in town in the category of "service with a smile." Their motif is riverboat gambling, hence the nickname the "Ship on the Strip." Avoid Joe's Bayou Restaurant; we found the Cajun cookin' wantin'.

IMPERIAL PALACE AND CASINO

3535 Las Vegas Blvd. S., Las Vegas, NV 89109 (702/731-3311; 800/634-6441).

Rates: Moderate, with Expensive Suites.

Amenities: 7 restaurants; swimming pool with waterfall; lounge; health spa.

Features: Chinese theme throughout public areas and rooms, including the blue pagoda rooftop; dead rock-and-rollers revue (played by impersonators, of course); **Imperial Palace Auto Collection**; minister-in-residence for those taking a spur-o'-the-moment plunge; gambling school.

Casino Action: baccarat; blackjack; craps; keno; poker; roulette; slots; sports betting; video poker.

The Imperial's Chinese motif can be too much for many people, but if you're having a hard time booking a room at a more desirable hotel, they've got 2,632 basic, decent rooms. Their permanent auto show has some pretty cool cars from yesteryear, including one of Der Fuehrer's cars and one built for a former King of Siam; the "Legends in Concert" show (the rock impersonator thing) varies from the sublime to the slimed, but that holds true for most Vegas production shows.

The sports betting complex here is very extensive, and gets high marks from the pros. The other games here are typical Vegas fare. Oddly enough given their Chinese theme, many visitors we talked to rated the Chinese food here well below par. We agree.

MAXIM HOTEL AND CASINO

160 E. Flamingo Rd., Las Vegas, NV 89109 (702/731-4300; 800/634-6987).

Rates: Moderate.

Amenities: 4 restaurants; swimming pool; shops; 2 lounges with live entertainment.

Features: comedy club; showroom.

Casino Action: baccarat; Big Six Wheel; blackjack; craps; keno; poker; slots; sports betting; video poker.

Set two blocks off the Strip, Maxim's claim to fame could well be the odd decor shared by each and every one of Maxim's 800 rooms: one of your walls will have silver foil covering it. Why? Because it's Las Vegas. The casino attracts good gamblers, particularly for poker and blackjack.

PALACE STATION HOTEL AND CASINO

2411 W. Sahara Ave., Las Vegas, NV 89102 (702/367-2411; 800/634-3101).

Rates: Moderate.

Amenities: 4 restaurants (one of them a great all-you-can-eat buffet); 2 pools; 2 Jacuzzis; lounge acts; gift shop; beauty salon; barber shop.

Features: free shuttle service to the Strip; big casino.

Casino Action: bingo; blackjack; craps; keno; poker; slots; sports betting; video poker.

Just west of the Strip, the Palace Station wants you to think railroad. That's their motif, and Amtrak should be proud. The Palace Station is one of the local favorites; 70 percent of the gamblers in here are Vegans. The 1,030 rooms are nice but nothing special. Even if you're not staying here, check out the excellent buffet. The casino is loaded with slot machines, with payoffs as high as a cool mil.

RIVIERA HOTEL AND CASINO

2901 Las Vegas Blvd. S., Las Vegas, NV 89109 (702/734-5110; 800/634-6753).

Rates: Moderate-to-Expensive.

Amenities: 5 restaurants and a fast-food food court; 2 swimming pools; Jacuzzi; 10 lit tennis courts; health spa; 4 showrooms; beauty salon; barber shop; shopping arcade; babysitting services.

Features: **Mardi Gras Showroom** featuring sexy shows for grown-ups; the aquatic *Splash* revue in the **Versailles Theater**; full-service business center; big casino; **Royale Wedding Chapel**.

Casino Action: blackjack; craps; slots; sports betting; video poker.

One of the founding fathers along the Strip, the Riviera has 2,136 rooms which live up to their deluxe billing. The restaurants are good values, if not great food, and the shows a lot of fun (in addition to those recommended above, check out the female impersonators). Good shows are a tradition here, since the immortal (well, immortal for Vegas) Liberace opened here nearly thirty years ago. The casino has no peer in terms of sheer size (125,000 square feet - although the MGM Grand casino opening next year will beat it by roughly 50,000 more square feet).

The Riviera gets high marks by one and all for design and comfort.

SAHARA HOTEL AND CASINO

2535 Las Vegas Blvd. S., Las Vegas, NV 89109 (702/737-2111; 800/634-6411).

Rates: Moderate.

Amenities: 6 restaurants, including a coffee shop and a buffet; 2 swimming pools; lounge acts; kids' video arcade;

shopping arcade; beauty salon.

Features: daycare; **Space Center** convention hall.

Casino Action: baccarat; blackjack; craps; keno; poker; roulette; slots; sports betting; video poker.

The Sahara marks the northern end of the Strip, or at least the old northern end (many now place Bob Stupak's Vegas World as the official "end") and is therefore convenient to Downtown. It too is one of the oldest hotels on the Strip, dating from 1952 (ancient history by Vegas standards). The best of the 2,035 rooms are in the tower and in the original bungalows. The casino is popular, and is usually pretty crowded. Their convention hall has become a popular meetings venue for those conventions with smaller needs.

SAN REMO CASINO AND RESORT

115 E. Tropicana Ave., Las Vegas, NV 89109 (702/739-9000; 800/522-7366).

Rates: Moderate.

Amenities: 5 restaurants; swimming pool; 2 lounges, one with big name acts; health spa; gift shop.

Features: crystal chandeliers in casino; well-appointed rooms and location near airport perfect for business travelers.

Casino Action: baccarat; Big Six Wheel; blackjack; craps; keno; Pai Gow; poker; roulette; slots; video poker.

The San Remo is an elegant Ramada hotel, designed not to look like other Ramadas you may have seen around but rather like its Italian namesake in the port of Genoa. The 711 rooms are plush, most of them completed just recently in the tower addition. The San Remo is located near the airport, at the southern end of the Strip.

SANDS HOTEL AND CASINO

3355 Las Vegas Blvd. S., Las Vegas, NV 89109 (702/733-5000; 800/446-4678).

Rates: Moderate.

Amenities: 4 restaurants (including a deli); 2 swimming pools; 6 lit tennis courts; 9-hole putting green; health spa; lounge acts; shopping; shuffleboard.

Features: good shows at the **Copa Room**; huge convention space.

Casino Action: baccarat; Big Six Wheel; blackjack; craps; keno; Pai Gow; roulette; slots; sports betting; video poker.

The Sands opened just two weeks after the Sahara around Christmas 1952. The Rat Packers (Sinatra, Dean Martin, Sammy Davis, Jr., etc.) used the Sands as one of their main bases, since Frankie and Deano each owned a nice piece of the pie.

Today, the Sands is still known for the great acts that appear in the famous Copa Room. The hotel has also become one of the top convention sites in town, sponsoring a number of top-flight gatherings. There are more than 720 rooms, with those in the tower more spacious and, obviously, more expensive.

SHEFFIELD INN

3970 Paradise Rd., Las Vegas, NV 89109 (702/796-9000; 800/777-1700).

Rates: Moderate.

Amenities: every room equipped with VCR, satellite TV, and whirlpool tub for two; swimming pool; volleyball, badminton, croquet.

Features: airport shuttle service; free Continental breakfast; hot tub; conference and meeting facilities for up to 100 people.

Casino Action: None.

Located a few blocks from the Strip, the Sheffield Inn does not have gambling, but they do have 228 very nice rooms and suites. The location near the airport and major Strip attractions makes it a good choice for business travelers or those less interested in gambling.

THE STARDUST HOTEL AND CASINO

3000 Las Vegas Blvd. S., Las Vegas, NV 89109 (702/732-6111; 800/634-6033).

Rates: Moderate.

Amenities: 7 restaurants, including a coffee shop, good buffet, and snack bar; 2 swimming pools; 4 bars and cocktail lounges; shopping arcade; extensive sports club; three 18-hole golf courses (reached via shuttle); kids' video arcade.

Features: **Enter the Night** production show at the **Stardust Theater**; RV park.

Casino Action: baccarat; bingo; blackjack; craps; keno; poker; roulette; slots; sports betting; video poker.

The Stardust, dating from 1959, underwent a $300 million expansion in 1991 and now boasts 2,300 rooms, most of which are large and comfortable. The all-you-can-eat buffet is one of the better ones, and their steak house, William B's, is one of the best joints in town. The "Enter the Night" show has become one of the 2 or 3 most popular shows, and tickets are hard to come by. The location is central, and the casino is very nice.

ST. TROPEZ HOTEL

455 E. Harmon St., Las Vegas, NV 89109 (702/369-5400; 800/666-5400).

Rates: Moderate-to-Expensive.

Amenities: restaurant; lounge; swimming pool; health spa.

Features: free buffet breakfast; shopping mall adjacent.
Casino Action: none.

The St. Tropez is about five minutes off the Strip, which makes sense since the hotel has no casino. But the rooms (mostly suites) are very nice, done up in Southwestern decor, and are reasonably priced considering the quality. If you're in town for a convention and are not interested in gambling, this would be a good pick, given its convenience to the Convention Center.

TROPICANA RESORT AND CASINO

3801 Las Vegas Blvd. S., Las Vegas, NV 89109 (702/739-2222; 800/634-4000).
Rates: Moderate.
Amenities: 10 restaurants, including coffee shops and snack bars; 3 swimming pools; 3 Jacuzzis; 4 lit tennis courts; 18-hole golf course; putting green; health spa; lounge acts; shops.
Features: **Tiffany Theater's** "Folies Bergere" adult extravaganza; generally good comedy club; the casino is covered by a stained-glass dome.
Casino Action: baccarat; blackjack; craps; keno; Pai Gow; poker; roulette; slots; sports betting; video poker.

Bring your lucky Hawaiian shirt to the refurbished Tropicana. Always one of the flashiest joints on the Strip (its nickname for years was the "Tiffany of the Strip"), the Tropicana remains a must-see. Island gods and other assorted tropical decor greets you as you enter. Out back, the pools, lagoons, jacuzzis, and 100-foot waterslide will keep you cool no matter how hot it gets (and you can play blackjack in one corner of the pool if you miss the action in the casino!). For our money, the "Folies Bergere" show is one of the best in town.

The hotel sits at the southern end of the Strip, across from Excalibur. The 1,913 rooms are decorated in Polynesian splendor and are quite nice. The casino has the most unique ceiling in town, but that green-and-red flowery rug is too much.

WESTWARD HO MOTEL AND CASINO

2900 Las Vegas Blvd. S., Las Vegas, NV 89109 (702/731-2900; 800/634-6803).
Rates: Moderate.
Amenities: 3 restaurants, including a deli and a buffet; 7 swimming pools; rooms come with Jacuzzis; lounge acts.
Features: airport shuttle; foreign exchange counter in lobby.
Casino Action: Big Six Wheel; blackjack; craps; keno; roulette; slots; video poker.

Well located in the middle of the Strip, Westward Ho calls itself the largest motel in the world, and, while that may be true, its casino does not offer as much as most others on the Strip. The big game here is slots, so if you've come to plunk quarters in the machines, you're in good shape. There are 1,000 rooms with parking right out in front.

Inexpensive

ALGIERS HOTEL

2845 Las Vegas Blvd. S., Las Vegas, NV 89109 (702/735-3311; 800/732-3361).
Rates: Inexpensive.
Amenities: 1 restaurant; swimming pool.
Features: video poker bar; wedding chapel; near Wet n' Wild.
Casino Action: None.

Algiers is a small hotel with 105 modest rooms. There is no casino, but its location on the Strip makes it convenient if you want to stroll to several big casinos nearby. Situated across the street from Circus Circus and not far from Wet n' Wild, Algiers is a good choice for families who can't get into Circus Circus or who are just not in the mood for constant carnivalia.

ARIZONA CHARLIE'S

740 S. Decatur Blvd., Las Vegas, NV 89107 (702/258-5200;800/842-2695).

Rates: Inexpensive.

Amenities: 3 restaurants, including an all-you-can-eat buffet; swimming pool; video arcade.

Features: bowling alley with 50 lanes; Country & Western bar; smoke-free casino.

Casino Action: bingo; blackjack; craps; slots; sports betting; video keno and video poker.

Arizona Charlie's is not right on the Strip, but it's not far away. With 100 rooms, it's one of the smaller hotels, but plans are underway for another 200 rooms. This is one of the local favorites, in part because of the casino's relatively non-glitzy atmosphere. The big money does not roll in here often, which is fine for most of the patrons. If you like to bowl, and if you like C&W music, you'll enjoy this no-frills joint.

BARBARY COAST HOTEL AND CASINO

3595 Las Vegas Blvd. S., Las Vegas, NV 89109 (702/737-7111; 800/634-6755).

Rates: Inexpensive.

Amenities: 3 restaurants; lounge acts; no swimming pool or big showroom.

Features: **Michael's** restaurant one of the city's best; America's biggest stained-glass mural; plenty of chandeliers.

Casino Action: baccarat; blackjack; craps; keno; poker; roulette; slots; sports betting; video poker.

The obscurely-named Barbary Coast (you trivia buffs will of course know that the Barbary Coast does not refer to North African piracy, but rather a district of old San Francisco noted for its bordellos and gambling houses; it was destroyed in the earthquake of 1906). It is indeed reminiscent of a Victorian-era San Francisco hotel. But there are plenty of pirates around - at the blackjack and other gaming tables.

The 198 rooms here are done up in late 19th-century San Francisco style, but the conveniences are late 20th-century. The Barbary Coast is a good choice if you want to be centrally located, or if you want to engage in (or just watch) some high-stakes gambling.

BOARDWALK HOTEL AND CASINO

3750 Las Vegas Blvd. S., Las Vegas, NV 89109 (702/735-1167; 800/635-4581).

Rates: Inexpensive.

Amenities: 2 restaurants; 2 swimming pools; bar.

Features: Elvis impersonator show in the lounge; Fun Book.

Casino Action: blackjack; Big Six; roulette; slots; video poker.

The Boardwalk is an older place, with a run-down look, but the casino is friendly and the 202 rooms are cheap. The showroom is a good place to catch Elvis, but other than that, the Boardwalk's location on the Strip is its best feature.

BOURBON STREET HOTEL AND CASINO

120 E. Flamingo, Las Vegas, NV 89109 (702/737-7200; 800/634-6956).

Rates: Inexpensive.

Amenities: buffet dining.

Features: Dixieland jazz music; free lounge acts; blackjack aces on the loose.

Casino Action: blackjack; craps; keno; roulette; poker; slots; video poker.

Bourbon Street is another small hotel and casino, located right near the Strip, but is beloved of those who enjoy an old-fashioned smoke-filled gambling house. As the name implies, the atmosphere is redolent of New Orleans, and it features Dixieland jazz to drive home the point. The 166 rooms are okay, but nothing special.

CIRCUS CIRCUS

2880 Las Vegas Blvd. S., Las Vegas, NV 89109 (702/734-0410; 800/634-3450).

Rates: Inexpensive.

Amenities: 8 restaurants and snack bars; 3 swimming pools; shops.

Features: geared for children; big-time free circus entertainment all day; **Carnival Midway** (carnival fun for kids of all ages); large RV park on premises; wedding chapel.

Casino Action: blackjack; craps; keno; poker; roulette; slots (several thousand machines!); sports betting; video blackjack, video poker; no-smoking section.

Bigtop PeeWee meets Nick the Greek at Circus Circus, and the result is, well, a wild kids' ride that has somehow gotten out of control. But it's one heck of a show. If you can handle gambling in a very noisy casino sculpted like a tent, with trapeze acts whizzing above, be our guest.

Circus Circus is actually great for families. It's an immense playland, with 2,800 brightly-colored rooms. The gambling here is more easygoing than many other places, since the focus is on kids and razzle-dazzle carnivalia. The "Grand Slam Canyon" is the newest attraction, a $75 million indoor roller coaster, water flume ride, lagoons, and more, all housed in a pink dome!

CONTINENTAL HOTEL CASINO AND RESORT
4100 Paradise Rd., Las Vegas, NV 89109 (702/737-5555; 800/634-6641).
Rates: Inexpensive.
Amenities: 2 restaurants (one is a buffet); 1 swimming pool; gift shop;
Features: babysitting services; handicapped-friendly; lounge acts (including daily comedy routines).
Casino Action: bingo; blackjack; craps; keno; poker; roulette; slots; video poker; sports betting.

Not far from the Strip, the Continental has 400 rooms from which to choose. The main gambling action here really is slots. If you want a comedic break from dropping nickels and quarters into machines, visit the lounge for the afternoon comedy act.

GOLD COAST HOTEL AND CASINO
4000 W. Flamingo Rd. Las Vegas, NV 89103 (702/367-7111; 800/331-5334).
Rates: Inexpensive.
Amenities: 5 restaurants; 2 movie theaters; free daycare and ice cream bar; 2 lounges.
Features: biggest Country-Western dance hall in the state; frequent shuttles to the Strip (just a few minutes away); 72-lane bowling alley.

Casino Action: baccarat; bingo; blackjack; craps; keno; Pai Gow; poker; roulette; slots.

Owned by the Barbary Coast Hotel folks, the Gold Coast is a good choice for families who don't want all the hoopla of Circus Circus or Excalibur. The Gold Coast is a great place to learn how to dance Country & Western style. Set off the Strip, the Gold Coast has 750 rooms and a huge casino area.

VEGAS WORLD

2000 Las Vegas Blvd. S., Las Vegas, NV 89104 (702/382-2000; 800/634-6277).
Rates: Inexpensive.
Amenities: 2 restaurants; 2 lounges; swimming pool; shops; kids' video arcade; beauty salon;
Features: outer space motif; attractive package deals featuring cash, chips, and gifts; big production showroom with name acts; Fun Book.
Casino Action: biggest Big Six (Wheel of Fortune) in town; blackjack; craps; keno; roulette; slots; video poker.

"Bob Stupak's Vegas World Hotel and Casino" is the full name, and the world he has built here is a celestial fantasy with moons, spaceships, and other astro-strangeness. Depending on your point of view, it's either a fun dream come true, or just a bad dream. Nightly Elvis and Sinatra impersonators are fairly popular attractions, as are Ed Sullivan Show comedians "Allen and Rossi."

The casino offers the largest jackpot on display ($1 million in cash - don't drool too much). Located at the northern edge of the Strip, Vegas World has 1,000 rooms. Plans call for a Stratosphere Tower which, at 1,012 feet, will be the tallest such structure in America.

RECOMMENDED MOTELS
- **Aztec Inn**, 2200 Las Vegas Blvd. S. (702/385-4566).
- **Best Western McCarran Inn**, 4970 Paradise Rd. (702/798-5530; 800/626-7575). As the name implies, this Best Western is right near the airport.
- **Center Strip Inn**, 3688 Las Vegas Blvd. S. (702/798-3090; 800/777-7737).
- **Days Inn**, 3265 Las Vegas Blvd. S. (702/735-5102).
- **Howard Johnson Tropicana**, 3311 W. Tropicana Ave (702/798-1111; 800/654-2000). Not far from the Strip.
- **Rodeway Inn**, 3786 Las Vegas Blvd. S. (702/736-1434).
- **Travelodge Center Strip**, 3419 Las Vegas Blvd. S. (702/734-6801).

CASINO-ONLY ESTABLISHMENTS
You might want to visit a few casinos not attached to hotels. If sports betting is your thing, start with **Little Caesar's Gambling Casino** at 3665 Las Vegas Blvd. S. (702/734-2827), a small, no-frills gambling joint. Inside you'll find gamblers smoking cigars and placing bets on races, ballgames, boxing matches, people crossing the Strip in heavy traffic and just about anything else. Available games are blackjack; craps; slots; sports betting; video blackjack; video keno; video poker. Bob Stupak of Vegas World Hotel fame bet and won $1 million here on the 1989 Super Bowl.

Four other casinos worth checking out on or near the Strip are:
- **Mahoney's Silver Nugget**, 2140 Las Vegas Blvd. N. (702/399-1111), with a restaurant and a good selection of games.
- **Town Hall Casino**, 4155 Koval Ln. (702/731-2111), a smaller place with a restaurant, bar, and entertainment.
- **Silver City Casino**, 3001 Las Vegas Blvd. S. (702/732-

4152), across the street from the Stardust Hotel.

- **Slots-A-Fun** (702/734-0410) located right on the Strip next to its owner, Circus Circus. Don't be fooled by the name; in addition to slots, Slots-A-Fun offers blackjack; craps; Pai Gow poker; poker; and Red Dog.

THE LATEST AND GREATEST RESORTS

Is Las Vegas becoming a desert Orlando? The hotel and theme park boom continues unabated on the Strip. Judging by the kinds of hotels going up, the casino operators are betting heavily that Vegas and theme parks are a match made in heaven. The competition for your vacation dollar is already stiff; with the addition of these new hotels and attractions, it's getting even stiffer.

Two of the three hotel/casinos going up - Luxor and MGM - are located on the southern end of the Strip (corner of Tropicana and Las Vegas Blvd. S.), further broadening the appeal of this part of town.

Circus Circus Enterprises is adding two new attractions to its Vegas money making machine with the Grand Slam Canyon rides behind Circus Circus Hotel and the Luxor Hotel and Casino next to Excalibur (also a Circus Circus property). When it comes to family fun in this town, nobody has an edge on these folks.

Here's what they're all about:

GRAND SLAM CANYON

The just-opened, $75 million, pink dome-enclosed Grand Slam Canyon, situated adjacent to Circus Circus, features lagoons, waterfalls, a water-flume ride, a four-loop roller coaster, shops, special-effects theaters, and restaurants set against a backdrop of Grand Canyon-esque scenes (grottoes, Anasazi villages). Enter from the casino's west end.

LUXOR HOTEL AND CASINO

3900 Las Vegas Blvd. S., Las Vegas, NV 89119 (702/262-4000; 800/288-1000).

Rates: Expensive.

Casino Action: baccarat; blackjack; craps; keno; Pai Gow; poker; roulette; slots; sports betting; video poker.

The $300 million Luxor, scheduled to open in October 1993 next door to the Excalibur Hotel, is shaped like a 30-story bronze-reflective pyramid and will have its very own Nile River snaking past a recreation of King Tut's Tomb through the atrium. There will be 2,521 rooms (including 14 suites), each with a balcony facing inward to overlook the largest hotel atrium in the world (29 million cubic feet).

A Nile riverboat will take you from registration to the elevators, which are also unique, as the ride up slants on a 39-degree angle. But you won't know it or feel any different due to the wonders of new - in this case microwave - technology. There will be seven theme restaurants, a showroom seating 1,200 and a flight-simulator-like ride.

MGM GRAND HOTEL AND THEME PARK

3799 Las Vegas Blvd. S., Las Vegas, NV 89109 (702/891-1111; 800/929-1111).

Rates: Expensive.

Casino Action: baccarat; blackjack; craps; keno; Pai Gow; poker; roulette; slots; sports betting; video poker.

On the same corner, across the street from Excalibur, will be the incredibly expensive MGM Grand, coming in at a cool bil (as in $1 billion!). Kirk Kerkorian, who owns the MGM Grand, is counting on at least one out of ten visitors to Vegas to walk through their doors to make back their money. It's due to open in February 1994 with 5,009 rooms (of which 744 will be suites) and so will have more rooms than any other resort hotel in the world.

The Theme Park will follow the hotel by several months. Twelve rides are planned, six for kids and six for adults. The main theme in the park will be famous city streets from around the world, past and present, but there will be other motifs too. The biggest attraction could well be Emerald City. A Special Events Arena seating 15,000; four theaters; a showroom seating 1,700; a big midway with games; a motion machine movie similar to Excalibur's; food; and shops round out MGM's gigantic project. Last but certainly not least, the casino will be the largest anywhere at 171,500 square feet, and will offer all games.

TREASURE ISLAND

3300 Las Vegas Blvd. S., Las Vegas, NV 89109 (702/894-7111; 800/944-7444).
Rates: Moderate.
Casino Action: baccarat; blackjack; craps; keno; Pai Gow; poker; roulette; slots; sports betting; video poker.

Steve Wynn, CEO of Mirage Resorts, is building the $430 million **Treasure Island**, slated to open its doors next to the Mirage Hotel in November 1993.

Treasure Island will be both a fun-park, casino, and mega-hotel with 3,000 rooms.

The theme here is Pirates of the Caribbean, and the rooms will be moderately-priced. The Cirque du Soleil, now at Mirage, will move to Treasure Island. Every hour, the pirate ship "Hispaniola" and the British battleship "HMS Sir Francis Drake" will fire their mighty cannons at each other, with live actors thrown into the fracas for good measure. By the way, the pirates will win each time!

DOWNTOWN HOTELS AND CASINOS

Expensive

GOLDEN NUGGET OF LAS VEGAS

129 E. Fremont St., Las Vegas, NV 89101 (702/385-7111; 800/634-3403).

Rates: Expensive.

Amenities: 4 restaurants, including a buffet; 1 showroom with name acts; lounge; swimming pool; shops; health spa; beauty salon.

Features: ornate decor featuring marble, stained and etched glass, chandeliers, Persian rugs, gold trim; **The Hand of Faith Nugget**, the largest solid gold nugget on public display in the world (weighing in at 875 troy oz., or 61 lbs., 11 oz).

Casino Action: baccarat; Big Six Wheel; blackjack; craps; keno; Pai Gow; poker; roulette; slots; sports betting; video poker.

Until 1977, the Golden Nugget was a gambling hall only; now it is the largest and most lavish hotel Downtown, with 1,907 sumptuous rooms and suites. The elegant restaurants are among the better ones in town. One of Las Vegas's classiest joints, the casino is bright and airy and is a favorite of both beginners and pros alike.

Moderate

FOUR QUEENS HOTEL AND CASINO

202 E. Fremont St., Las Vegas, NV 89101 (702/385-4011; 800/634-6045).

Rates: Moderate.

Amenities: 3 restaurants, including an ice cream parlor; gift

DOWNTOWN LAS VEGAS MAP

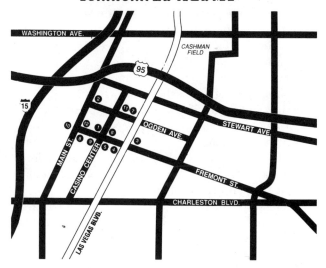

1. Binion's Horseshoe
2. California
3. El Cortez
4. Fitzgerald's
5. Four Queens
6. Fremont
7. Gold Spike
8. Golden Gate
9. Golden Nugget
10. Jackie Gaughan's Plaza
11. Lady Luck
12. Las Vegas Club

shop; kids' video and game arcade; lounge acts.

Features: **Ripley's Believe It Or Not Museum**; world's largest slot machine (this thing is huge!).

Casino Action: baccarat; Big Six Wheel; blackjack; craps; keno; poker; roulette; slots; video poker.

"Four Queens" has a double meaning: one used for card players, the other for the owner's four daughters. The hotel has 720 rooms decorated in an updated version of Victoriana. It is well known for its New Orleans-style jazz musicians appearing in the lounge every Monday night. The Ripley's Believe It Or Not Museum has got an interesting, fun, and unusual collection of oddities (gamblers will love the big jelly-bean roulette wheel).

The slots in the casino at Four Queens offer a payoff of up to $1 million. This is another of the favorite haunts of prowling blackjack aces.

JACKIE GAUGHAN'S PLAZA HOTEL AND CASINO

1 Main St., Las Vegas, NV 89101 (702/386-2110; 800/634-6575).

Rates: Moderate.

Amenities: 4 restaurants, including a snack bar and coffee shop; lounge acts; big-name showroom; exercise facilities and jogging track; four lit tennis courts; numerous shops; beauty salon; barber shop; video games; ice cream shop.

Features: located right above the train station; adjacent Greyhound bus station; wedding chapel; huge indoor and outdoor parking lot.

Casino Action: baccarat; blackjack; craps; keno; Pai Gow; poker; roulette; slots; sports betting; video blackjack, video poker.

Formerly the Union Plaza, Jackie Gaughan's Plaza

Hotel has a great location for those coming to town by rail. The hotel's 1,037 modern, bright rooms makes it one of Downtown's biggest, best hostelries, but ask for a room facing Fremont Street unless you dig a view of train tracks.

The Plaza offers two things that no other Downtown hotel does: tennis and big-time shows. Because the casino caters to beginners and those seeking low-minimum betting, it tends to get pretty crazy in there. The **Centerstage Restaurant** is noteworthy not so much for its steaks, but for the great neon-view of Glitter Gulch.

LADY LUCK CASINO AND HOTEL

206 N. Third St., Las Vegas, NV 89101 (702/477-3000; 800/523-9582).

Rates: Moderate.

Amenities: 6 restaurants, including a coffee shop, snack bar, and buffet; swimming pool; gift shop; Showroom with big acts; impressive dance floor; long-running magic show (recently relocated to Lady Luck) *Melinda and her Follies Revue*.

Features: complementary airport shuttle; free gambling instruction; health club; all rooms have Jacuzzis; tremendous **Big Bertha** slot machine; blackjack tournaments; Fun Book.

Casino Action: baccarat; blackjack; craps; roulette; keno; Pai Gow; slots; video poker and video blackjack.

One of the few casinos in town that acknowledges (by virtue of their large windows) that there is a world out there beyond gambling. Originally a small slot joint, successive expansions have made the casino (and the hotel) a favorite of gambling pros and beginners alike.

All 796 rooms and suites have Jacuzzis, the restaurants

are quality affairs, and the room size and decor is comfortable and bright.

Inexpensive

BINION'S HORSESHOE CASINO AND HOTEL

128 Fremont St., Las Vegas, NV 89101 (702/382-1600; 800/937-6537).

Rates: Inexpensive-to-Moderate.

Amenities: 5 restaurants, including a coffee shop and a buffet; 1 bar, 1 lounge; swimming pool on roof; shops;

Features: the site of the **World Series of Poker**; display of $1 million in 100 $10,000 bills in the casino; **The Steak House** is one of the very better steak restaurants in Vegas; the **Skye Room** restaurant affords great panoramic views of the city.

Casino Action: baccarat; bingo; blackjack; craps; keno; poker; roulette; slots; sports betting; video poker.

Benny Binion's Horseshoe Hotel is a Las Vegas landmark. While Benny is no longer with us, the Binion family continues to run the place the old-fashioned way. The motif here is frontier Western, and the staff is one of the nicest in town. There are now 354 rooms (the ones in the older section have more character; the rooms in the tower have a great view), but the Horseshoe has always been better known as a fun, no-limit casino, which attracts a lot of high-stakes craps and poker players. Anyone with ten grand to spare can enter the internationally-renowned World Series of Poker.

THE CALIFORNIA HOTEL AND CASINO

12 Ogden Ave., Las Vegas, NV 89101 (702/385-1222; 800/634-6255).

Rates: Inexpensive.
Amenities: 4 restaurants, all good; 3 bars and a lounge with live acts; swimming pool; Jacuzzi; game room; shopping.
Features: 222-space RV park; daily slot tourney.
Casino Action: baccarat; blackjack; craps; keno; Pai Gow poker; roulette; slots; sports betting; video keno and video poker.

One of four hotel/casinos owned by Sam Boyd, the California boasts 650 large, cozy rooms and the only RV park in the Downtown area. There is a tropical look to the place, although not quite like the Tropicana or Rio. The swimming pool up top is very small. The restaurants are among the best hotel restaurants in Vegas. All in all, a friendly place with a good casino.

EL CORTEZ HOTEL AND CASINO

600 E. Fremont St., Las Vegas, NV 89109 (702/385-5200; 800/634-6703).
Rates: Inexpensive.
Amenities: 2 restaurants; shopping; snack bar; kid's game room; 2 bars.
Features: oldest remaining casino in town; Fun Book.
Casino Action: baccarat; blackjack; craps; keno; poker; roulette; slots; sports betting; video keno and video poker.

El Cortez, built in 1941, is the oldest remaining casino in Las Vegas. The 308 rooms are small and simple, but they're among the cheapest in town. A favorite of senior citizens and tour groups, El Cortez is famous for its easy slot machines. Part of the original adobe structure still stands.

FITZGERALD'S HOTEL AND CASINO

301 E. Fremont St., Las Vegas, NV 89101 (702/388-2400; 800/274-5825)

Rates: Inexpensive-to-Moderate.
Amenities: 2 restaurants; 1 coffee shop; plenty of parking; health facilities; gift shop; lounge acts.
Features: **Lucky Forest**, a room with lucky objects; tallest building in Nevada (great view from the top); gambling instruction; tasty Italian food at **Chicago Joe's**; Fun Book.
Casino Action: bingo; blackjack; craps; keno; roulette; slots; video poker and video slots. NOTE: there is a no-smoking slots section.

At 33 stories, Fitzgerald's is housed in the biggest building in the state, but with 650 rooms it doesn't hold a candle to the mega-resorts on the Strip. Still, it has more rooms than most other Downtown hotels. The theme at Fitzgerald's, as you might guess from the name, is Irish and green, from green rugs to green shamrocks to green four-leaf clovers. The casino is sizable and offers most games; some slots are advertised as giving a 101% payback.

FREMONT HOTEL AND CASINO

200 E. Fremont St., Las Vegas, NV 89101 (702/385-3232; 800/634-6182).
Rates: Inexpensive.
Amenities: 4 restaurants (including an all-you-can-eat buffet); lounge acts; gift shop.
Features: good dining.
Casino Action: bingo; blackjack; craps; keno; Pai Gow; poker; slots; sports betting; video poker.

Opened in 1956, Sam Boyd's Fremont is beloved by locals, in part because the casino has an older, darker, less modern-glitz feel. Vegas history buffs will want to know that the lounge at the Fremont was the launching pad for young Wayne Newton's crooning career. The hotel offers 452 decent-sized rooms.

GOLD SPIKE HOTEL AND CASINO

400 E. Ogden, Las Vegas, NV 89101 (702/384-8444; 800/634-6703).

Rates: Inexpensive.

Amenities: 1 restaurant; budget snack bar.

Features: cheap gambling; breakfast included.

Casino Action: bingo; keno (including keno machines); slots (including penny slots); video poker.

The Gold Spike is a small hotel, with 109 rooms, but is a good choice for those who want to gamble cheaply. The rooms are nothing special, but they are about the least expensive around. The bingo is free and you can still play penny slots here, but the casino is usually packed to the rafters.

GOLDEN GATE HOTEL AND CASINO

111 S. Main St., Las Vegas, NV 89101 (702/382-3510; 800/426-0521).

Rates: Inexpensive.

Amenities: 1 restaurant.

Features: Famous for its great 99¢ shrimp cocktail.

Casino Action: blackjack; craps; keno; slots; video poker.

The Golden Gate is another budget hotel with 106 relatively small rooms. Most come in here to play slots and blackjack, and devour what we consider the best 99¢ shrimp cocktail in town.

LAS VEGAS CLUB HOTEL AND CASINO

18 E. Fremont St., Las Vegas, NV 89101 (702/385-1664; 800/634-6532).

Rates: Inexpensive-to-Moderate.

Amenities: 2 restaurants, including a coffee shop; babysitting available.

Features: great old-time baseball collection in "Sports Hall of Fame."

Casino Action: blackjack; craps; keno; roulette; slots; sports betting; video blackjack and video poker.

Baseball is the main theme here (the name of the coffee shop is the "Dugout"), but other sports like boxing and basketball are played up too. As you'd expect from a sports joint, the restaurant is one of the better steak places in town. The 224 rooms are on the small side, but very nicely done in Southwestern colors. In the Sports Hall of Fame, you'll find their World Series Bat Collection (from 1946 through 1958), the bronzed shoes of baseball greats, autographed baseballs, and the life. The casino's liberal blackjack rules attract a lot of beginners, as well as those who just like the easy blackjack play.

RECOMMENDED MOTELS

- **Ambassador Motel**, 902 E. Fremont (702/384-8420).
- **Crest Budget Inn**, 207 N. 6th St. (702/382-5642; 800/777-1817).
- **Days Inn**, 707 E. Fremont (702/388-1400; 800/325-2344). Slot Parlor.
- **Econolodge Downtown**, 520 S. Casino Center Blvd. (702/384-8211; 800/223-7706).
- **Ogden House**, 651 Ogden Ave. (702/385-5200).
- **Western Hotel Bingo Parlor and Casino**, 899 E. Fremont (702/384-4620; 800/634-6703). Never mind the name, it's a motel. Bingo, blackjack, slots, poker, keno, roulette; video poker. Free breakfast.

CASINO-ONLY ESTABLISHMENTS

Two Downtown casinos with no hotel attached to them that are worthy of note:

- **Leroy's Horse and Sports Place**, 114 S. First Ave. (702/ 382-1561). Leroy's is a small affair offering sports betting only.
- **Pioneer Club**, First and Fremont (702/382-4576). The Pioneer Club has a buffet and offers blackjack, craps, keno, slots, video poker and video blackjack. Fun Book coupons redeemed here.

GREATER LAS VEGAS HOTELS AND CASINOS

Greater Las Vegas is often overlooked as a place to stay, but this part of town may be right for you if you want to escape from the more hectic pace on the Strip or the glitter of Downtown. There are no expensive hotels out this way, so we've started you off with the moderate places.

Moderate

MT. CHARLESTON HOTEL

2 Kyle Canyon Rd., Las Vegas, NV 89124 (702/872-5500).
Rates: Moderate.
Amenities: 1 restaurant; lounge; sauna; jacuzzi; lobby fireplace.
Features: Wedding and banquet facilities; lounge entertainment on weekend nights.
Casino Action: none, although there are a few keno and video poker machines.

The Mt. Charleston Hotel is a very pleasant affair with 63 sizable rooms and a few suites. The best feature is the location, in a canyon in the Toiyabe National Forest, within sight of 12,000-foot Mt. Charleston, the tallest peak in the Las Vegas Valley. If you're looking for a nice spot to have a wedding, the atmosphere is terrific here.

SAM'S TOWN HOTEL AND GAMBLING HALL

5111 Boulder Highway, Las Vegas, NV 89122 (702/456-7777; 800/634-6371).

Rates: Moderate.

Amenities: 5 restaurants, including a buffet; 10 bars and saloons, several with live Country & Western music; swimming pool; ice cream parlor.

Features: Old West theme; bowling alley; **Western Dance Hall**; big Western clothing and accessories store and other shops; RV park.

Casino Action: bingo; blackjack; craps; keno; poker; roulette; slots; sports betting; video blackjack and video poker.

Sam's Town is a fun, hootin', hollerin' kind of place. Kids will like it here (just make sure they only order sarsaparillas if they sneak into one of the many bars here). The Mexican food joint is good, as are the steaks at the steak house. The Western Dance Hall attracts many locals. The 197 rooms are a good value, and the casino offers standard action.

Inexpensive

GOLD STRIKE INN AND CASINO

Boulder Highway (US-93), Las Vegas, NV 89005 (702/293-5000; 800/245-6380).

Rates: Inexpensive-to-Moderate.

Amenities: 1 restaurant; lounge acts.

Features: many rooms overlook Lake Mead; good locale for day trips to Hoover Dam, Lake Mead Recreation Area.

Casino Action: blackjack; craps; poker; roulette; slots; video poker and video blackjack.

Ask for a lakeside room for a great view looking out over Lake Mead, just four miles from Hoover Dam. Gold

Strike has a colorful Old West theme, from the shops out in front to the casino and the 155 rooms. A good choice for those who want to hike or see more of the desert and local attractions than you can from inside a Strip casino.

NEVADA PALACE HOTEL AND CASINO

5255 Boulder Highway, Las Vegas, NV 89122 (702/458-8810; 800/634-6283).

Rates: Inexpensive.

Amenities: 3 restaurants, including one buffet.

Features: **Silverado Saloon and Dance Hall**.

Casino Action: Big Six (Wheel of Fortune); bingo; blackjack; craps; keno; poker; roulette; slots; video poker.

The Nevada Palace is a fun, down-to-earth casino, well-liked by locals and visitors on budgets. Like other hotel/casinos off the Strip (and especially those along Boulder Highway), this is a good choice if you don't want the noise and glitz. It's location is well-suited to day trips to Hoover Dam or Lake Mead. There are 220 rooms and three sizable suites.

RAILROAD PASS HOTEL AND CASINO

2800 S. Boulder Highway, Las Vegas, NV 89005 (702/294-5000; 800/654-0877).

Rates: Inexpensive.

Amenities: 1 restaurant; buffet; coffee shop; gift shop; video arcade; outdoor swimming pool.

Features: close to Hoover Dam; nice views.

Casino Action: blackjack; craps; keno; roulette; slots; video blackjack, video keno, and video poker.

The Railroad pass offers scenic vistas looking out at mountains on one side, and the valley southwest of Vegas on the other. Located just outside of Boulder City, the

Railroad Pass is another of the cheap but perfectly adequate hotel/casinos en route to Hoover Dam. The casino is relatively small.

SANTA FE HOTEL AND CASINO

4949 N. Rancho Dr., Las Vegas, NV 89130 (702/658-4900; 800/872-6823).

Rates: Inexpensive.

Amenities: 2 restaurants, one a buffet; jazz lounge.

Features: bowling alley with "Bowlervision;" the only regulation stadium ice skating/hockey rink in town.

Casino Action: blackjack; craps; keno; slots; video blackjack and video poker.

The Santa Fe is just a few years old, and is well off the beaten path in North Las Vegas. Decorated in Southwestern pastels, the owners have done an admirable job with the 200 rooms. For those craving some silence with a nice view of the mountains, this could be your spot. Unfortunately, there is no swimming pool.

SHOWBOAT HOTEL AND CASINO

2800 E. Fremont, Las Vegas, NV 89104 (702/385-9123; 800/826-2800).

Rates: Inexpensive.

Amenities: 3 restaurants, including a coffee shop; swimming pool; lit tennis courts; 18-hole golf course (reached by shuttle bus); beauty salon; barber shop; kids' video arcade; lounge acts.

Features: the 106-lane **Bowling Center**, site of many Pro Bowling tourneys; babysitting services; **Sports Pavilion**.

Casino Action: bingo; blackjack; craps; keno; Pai Gow; poker; roulette; slots; video poker.

The Showboat's patrons are loyal - they come back time

and again to this popular place. Bowlers the world over love the Showboat, and most families will too, offering babysitting services and a video games arcade. Opened in 1954, the Showboat retains its riverboat theme.

If you like to watch athletic contests, instead of participate in them, the Sports Pavilion is home to a number of professional boxing and wrestling matches. The 800 rooms at the Showboat are a good deal for the price. The casino also has a nifty bingo hall.

VACATION VILLAGE

6711 Las Vegas Blvd. S., Las Vegas, NV 89119 (702/897-1700; 800/658-5000).

Rates: Inexpensive; Suites are Moderate.

Amenities: 4 restaurants; 3 lounges and bars, with lounge acts; swimming pool; spa; shops.

Features: free shuttle service; Fun Book; cheapest draft beer around; nice Southwestern decor.

Casino Action: Big Six; blackjack; craps; Pai Gow poker; roulette; slots; video poker.

South of the Strip, Vacation Village has 313 inexpensively-priced rooms, of which eight are moderately-priced suites. Plans are underway to add 124 rooms. The pool is one of the nicest features here, with a good view of the surrounding desert. The casino offers most games.

RECOMMENDED MOTELS

- **Allstar Inns**, 4125 Boulder Highway, Las Vegas (702/457-8051).
- **Barcelona Motel**, 5011 E. Craig Rd. (702/644-6300; 800/223-6330). Slots.
- **Desert Inn of Boulder City**, 800 Nevada Highway, Boulder City (702/293-2827).

- **Meadows Inn**, 525 E. Bonanza Rd. (702/456-5600; 800/
  331-3504). Some games.
- **Moulin Rouge**, 900 W. Bonanza Rd. (702/648-5040).
- **Super 8 Motel**, *three locations:* 5288 Boulder Highway, Las
  Vegas (702/435-8888), with the **Longhorn Casino** at-
  tached; 4435 Las Vegas Blvd. N. (702/644-5666); 704
  Nevada Highway, Boulder City (702/294-8888).

LAKE LAS VEGAS DEVELOPMENT

*In Henderson, just outside of town, one of the largest
private development projects in the state, **Lake Las Vegas**
is now accepting offers to buy premium land right on the
manmade lake, which measures two miles long by one mile
wide. Get your bids in now: you only have until the year
2002 before the project is finished!*

*Jack Nicklaus has been brought in to design what will
be one of five professional-caliber golf courses. Six hotels and
more than 11,000 rooms are planned, along with stores
galore and 4,000 homes.*

And while not a motel, the **Boulder Dam Hotel** should
be included here with a special mention. Located in
Boulder City (1305 Arizona St., 702/293-1808), the hotel is
on the National Register of Historic Places. Well-preserved, the hotel is within striking distance of Hoover Dam
and Lake Mead, about 30-40 minutes southwest of town.

Another nice place to stay in the area near the Dam is
the **Lake Mead Lodge** (322 Lakeshore Rd., Boulder City,
702/293-2074). The Lodge is small, but the 42 rooms have
very attractive views of the Lake. Boating is available, and
their floating restaurant is popular with both tourists and
locals.

6. CASINO BASICS AND MONEY MANAGEMENT

•

CASINO BASICS

In this chapter we'll get you oriented to the casino gambling environment and show you the all-important techniques of money management.

Converting Traveller's Checks and Money Orders to Cash

The dealers accept only cash or chips at the table, so if you bring traveller's checks, money orders or the like, you must go to the area of the casino marked **Casino Cashier** to get these converted to cash. Be sure to bring proper identification to ensure a smooth transaction.

Casino Chips

Chip denominations run in $1, $5, $25, $100 and $500 units. If you're a big stakes player, you may even find $1,000, $2,500, $5,000 and $10,000 chips available!

The usual color scheme of chips is as follows: $1 chips are silver dollars, $5 chips will be red, $25 - green, and $100 - black. Chips of larger deniminations, such as $500 or $1,000, may be white, pink or other colors.

In casino parlance, $1 chips are generally referred to as *silver*, $5 chips as *nickels*, $25 chips as *quarters*, and

$100 chips as *dollars*. Unless playing at a 25¢ minimum craps table, $1 chips are the minimum currency used.

Betting

Casinos prefer that the player uses chips for betting purposes, for the handling of money at the tables is cumbersome and slows the game. However, cash can be used to bet with, though all payoffs will be in chips.

House Limits

The house limits will be posted on placards located on each corner of the table. They will indicate the minimum bet required to play and also the maximum bet allowed.

Minimum bets range from $1 and $5 per bet, to a maximum of $500, $1000 or $2,000 a bet. Occasionally, 25¢ tables may be found as well, but don't count on it. If special arrangements are made, a player can bet as much as he can muster in certain casinos. The Horseshoe Casino in Las Vegas is known to book any bet no matter the size.

In 1981, a man walked into the Horseshoe and placed a bet for $777,777. He bet the don't pass in craps, and walked out two rolls later with one and a half million dollars in cash!

Converting Chips into Cash

Dealers do not convert your chips into cash. Once you've bought your chips at the table, that cash is dropped into a dropbox, and thereafter is unobtainable. When you are ready to convert your chips back to cash, take them to the cashier's cage where the transaction will be done.

EYE IN THE SKY

Look above the playing area in any casino and you'll see dark, half-circle globes that look like light fixtures. What you're seeing is casino security in action, the ubiquitous "Eye in the Sky." The device is a one-way surveillance camera, used by security to ensure that no cheating occurs, either by players or dealers. Cameras are also located in other key spots in the casino, usually behind glass doors or walls. Considering that every conceivable kind of cheating has at one time or another been attempted in Las Vegas, the casinos have become pretty expert in spotting ne'er-do-wells.

But what you and I consider cheating sometimes differ from what the casino considers cheating. The biggest difference between the casinos and the players is over card counting in blackjack. Most players and experts argue that card counting is merely a way of regaining the edge the house has given itself in every hand. Gamblers argue that not counting is akin to a major league baseball player holding back on his slugging advantage, or not bagging a ball easily within reach. To the casino operators, card counting is cheating, pure and simple - so be careful if you're going to count!

Free Drinks and Cigarettes

Casinos offer their customers unlimited free drinking while gambling at the tables or slot machines. In addition to alcoholic beverages, a player can order milk, soft drinks, juices or any other beverages available. This is ordered through and served by a cocktail waitress.

Cigarettes and cigars are also complimentary and can be ordered through the same cocktail waitress.

Tipping

Tipping, or **toking**, as it is called in casino parlance, should be viewed as a gratuitous gesture by the player to the dealer or crew of dealers he feels has given him good service. Tipping is totally at the player's discretion, and in no way should be considered an obligation.

If you toke, toke only when you're winning, and only if the crew is friendly and helpful to you. Do not toke dealers that you don't like or ones that try to make you feel guilty about not tipping. Dealers that make playing an unpleasant experience for you deserve nothing.

MONEY MANAGEMENT

You trip to Las Vegas can be a great one, but only so long as you don't lose your shirt at the tables. Don't be one of those gamblers who, as the saying goes, drives into town in a $20,000 Cadillac and leaves in a $150,000 Greyhound bus.

To be a winner at gambling, you must exercise sound money management principles and keep your emotions under control. The temptation to ride a winning streak too hard in the hopes of a big killing, or to bet wildly during a losing streak, trying for a quick comeback, can spell doom. Wins can turn into losses, and moderate losses can turn into a nightmare.

Instead, one must plan ahead and prepare for the game. It's important to understand the nature of the gamble. In any gambling pursuit where luck plays a role, fluctuations in one's fortunes are common. It is the ability of the player to successfully deal with the ups and downs inherent in the gamble that separate the smart gamblers from the losers.

Here are the **three important principles** of money management:

1. Never gamble with money you cannot afford to lose either financially or emotionally.

Do not gamble with needed funds no matter how "sure" any bet seems. The possibilities of losing are real, and if that loss will hurt, you're playing the fool.

2. Bankroll yourself properly.

Undercapitalization leaves a player vulnerable in two ways. First, a normal downward trend can wipe out a limited money supply. Second, and more important, the bettor may feel pressured by the shortage of capital and play less powerfully than smart play dictates.

If the amount staked on a bet is above your head, you're playing in the wrong game. Play only at levels of betting you feel comfortable with.

3. Know when to quit - set stop-loss limits.

What often separates the winners from the losers is that the winners, when winning, leave the table a winner, and when losing, restrict their losses to affordable amounts. Smart gamblers never allow themselves to get destroyed at the gamble.

Minimizing losses is the key. You can't always win. If you're losing, keep the losses affordable - take a break. You only want to play with a clear head.

When you're winning big, put a good chunk of these winnings in a "don't touch" pile, and play with the rest. You never want to hand all your winnings back to the casino. Should a losing streak occur, you're out of there - a winner!!!

7. GAMBLING TO WIN!

You can win in Vegas! - sometimes with luck, sometimes with skill, but it is the smart player, the one who learns the skills necessary to win, that has the best chances of beating the house. In this chapter, we'll give you those basic skills and show you how to be a winner!

In **blackjack**, we'll show you the winning strategies that actually give you an edge over the casino; in **craps**, we show you the best bets to make, some of which give the casino no edge at all; in **keno**, you'll learn how to go for a $50,000 win; in **poker**, you'll learn to play and win at five variations; in **video poker**, how to get the edge over the machines; in **roulette**; how to make over 150 wagers; and in **slots**, we'll show you a few inside strategies for winning jackpots.

While no one can guarantee whether you'll win or lose you'll have the best chances to come home with money if you read this section carefully. Pay attention and good luck!

For your information: The legal gambling age is 21. And casinos do enforce the law!

Avery Cardoza is the best-selling writer of more than a dozen gambling books and strategies and the foremost gambling publisher in the world. No other living gambler/author has as much experience teaching the basics of the games, and most importantly how to win! He has prepared the following chapter with visitors to Las Vegas specifically in mind.

BLACKJACK

Blackjack can be beaten! With proper play, you can actually have the edge over the casino, and thus, the expectation to win money every time you play! In this section, we'll show you how to do just that - be a winner.

Object of the Game

The object of blackjack is to beat the dealer. This can be done by having a higher total than the dealer without exceeding 21 points or when the dealer's total exceeds 21, called **busting** (assuming the player hasn't busted first).

Decks of Cards - The Basics

Las Vegas casinos use one, two, four, six and sometimes as many as eight decks of cards in their blackjack games. Each deck used in blackjack is a standard pack of 52 cards. Suits have no relevance; only the numerical value of the cards count. Cards are counted at face value, 2 = 2 points, 3 = 3 points, except for the ace, which is valued at 1 or 11 points at the player's discretion, and the **picture cards,** the J, Q, K, all of which count as 10.

THE BLACKJACK LAYOUT

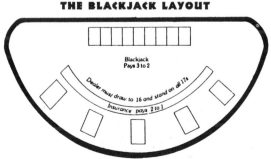

Entering a Game

To enter a blackjack game, sit down at any unoccupied seat at the blackjack table, and place the money you wish to gamble with near the betting box in front of you. The dealer will exchange your money for chips.

SINGLE DECK - HITTING AND STANDING

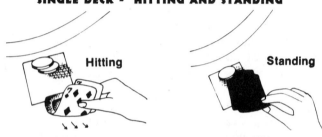

Hitting

Standing

MULTIPLE DECK - HITTING AND STANDING

Hitting

Standing

The Player's Options

Each player gets dealt two cards, as does the dealer, and after examining them and the one exposed dealer's card, the player has several options.

He can **stand,** take no more cards; **hit** or **draw,** take an additional card or cards; **double down,** double his bet and take one more card only; **split,** take cards of equal value and split them into two separate hands; or as is only sometimes offered, **surrender**, forfeit the hand along with half the bet.

A player may draw cards until he is satisfied with his total; however, once his total exceeds 21, his hand is **busted**, and he's a loser, regardless of what happens to the dealer's hand subsequently.

The Dealer's Rules

The dealer, however, has no such options, and must play by prescribed rules. Once the players have played out their hands, it's the dealer's turn. He turns over his hidden card for all to see, and must draw to any hand 16 or below and stand on any total 17-21. The dealer has no options and cannot deviate from these rules.

In some casinos the dealer must draw to a **soft** 17 - a total reached when the Ace is valued at 11 points.

Payoffs

The bettors play only against the dealer and must have a higher point total without exceeding 21 to win. Winning bets are paid at even money. When both hold the same total, it is a **push**, a tie, and nobody wins.

If the dealer busts, all remaining players (those who have not already busted) win and are paid out at **even money**, $1 paid for every $1 bet.

Players who get dealt a **blackjack**, an ace and any 10-value card (10, J, Q or K), get paid 3-2 unless the dealer gets a blackjack also, where it's a push. If the dealer gets a blackjack, he wins only what the player has bet.

Insurance

When the dealer shows an Ace as the exposed card, the player is offered an option called **Insurance**. It's a bet that the dealer has a 10-value card underneath for a black-jack. The player is allowed to bet up to one half of his original bet, and will get paid 2 to 1 if indeed he is correct. This is always a bad bet unless one is a card counter, and therefore should not be made.

Winning Strategies

Dealer Pat Hands: 7-Ace as Upcard - When the dealer shows a 7, 8, 9, 10 or Ace, hit all hard totals of 16 or less.

Dealer Stiffs: 2-6 as Upcard - When the dealer shows a 2, 3, 4, 5 or 6, cards he will frequently bust with, stand on all hard total of 12 or more. Do not bust against a dealer stiff card. Exception - Hit 12 vs. 2 or 3.

Player Totals of 11 or Less - On point totals of 11 or less, always draw (if you do not double or split).

Player Totals of Hard 17 or More - On point totals of hard 17 or more, stand.

Doubling and Splitting - Play aggressively, taking full advantage of doubling and splitting options, as presented in the master strategy chart on the following page.

THE MASTER STRATEGY CHART

The following Master Strategy Chart gives you an extremely accurate game against both single and multiple deck games in Las Vegas. For single deck games, make the plays as shown. For multiple deck games, where there is an asterisk, hit only - do not double or split.

BLACKJACK: MASTER STRATEGY CHART

Player's Hand	- Dealer's Upcard -									
	2	3	4	5	6	7	8	9	10	A
7/less	H	H	H	H	H	H	H	H	H	H
8	H	H	H	H	H	H	H	H	H	H
9	D*	D	D	D	D	H	H	H	H	H
10	D	D	D	D	D	D	D	D	H	H
11	D	D	D	D	D	D	D	D	D	D*
12	H	H	S	S	S	H	H	H	H	H
13	S	S	S	S	S	H	H	H	H	H
14	S	S	S	S	S	H	H	H	H	H
15	S	S	S	S	S	H	H	H	H	H
16	S	S	S	S	S	H	H	H	H	H
A2	H	H	D*	D	D	H	H	H	H	H
A3	H	H	D*	D	D	H	H	H	H	H
A4	H	H	D	D	D	H	H	H	H	H
A5	H	H	D	D	D	H	H	H	H	H
A6	D*	D	D	D	D	H	H	H	H	H
A7	S	D	D	D	D	S	S	H	H	H
A8	S	S	S	S	S	S	S	S	S	S
A9	S	S	S	S	S	S	S	S	S	S
22	H	spl*	spl	spl	spl	spl	H	H	H	H
33	H	H	spl	spl	spl	spl	H	H	H	H
44	H	H	H	H	H	H	H	H	H	H
55	D	D	D	D	D	D	D	D	H	H
66	spl	spl	spl	spl	spl	H	H	H	H	H
77	spl	spl	spl	spl	spl	spl	H	H	H	H
88	spl	spl	spl	spl	spl	spl	spl	spl	spl	spl
99	spl	spl	spl	spl	spl	S	spl	spl	S	S
1010	S	S	S	S	S	S	S	S	S	S
AA	spl	spl	spl	spl	spl	spl	spl	spl	spl	spl

H = Hit   S = Stand   D= Double   spl = Split
*In multiple deck games, hit only - do not double or split.

CRAPS

Craps is the most exciting of the casino games, for the action is fast, and a player catching a good roll can win large sums of money quickly. In this section we'll show you how to make the best bets available and be a winner.

Entering a Game

To enter a craps game, slip into a space by the rail of the craps table. After catching the dealer's attention, you can exchange your cash for chips.

The Basics

Craps is played with two standard six-sided dice, with each die numbered from 1 to 6. Bets are placed on a craps **layout**, a large green felt which is marked with the various bets possible and on which the dice are thrown.

The Come-Out Roll

The first roll of the dice is called the **come-out roll.** It marks the first roll of the **shoot** and can become either an automatic winner or loser for **pass line** bettors - players betting with the dice, or **don't pass bettors**, those betting against the dice; or the roll can establish a point.

If the come-out roll is an automatic decision, a 2, 3, 7, 11 or 12, the affected players will have their bets paid or lost, and the following roll will be a new come-out roll.

Any other number thrown, a 4, 5, 6, 8, 9 or 10 becomes the **point**.

Pass Line Bet

The throw of a 7 or 11 on the come-out roll is an automatic winner, while the throw of a **craps,** a 2, 3, or 12 is an automatic loser. Any other number is the point.

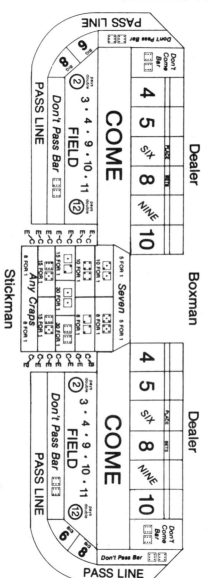

Nevada Craps Layout

Pass line bets win if the point repeats before the 7 and lose if the 7 is thrown first. All other throws are immaterial. A winning bet pays even money. Pass line bets are made by placing the wager in the area marked *Pass Line.*

Don't Pass Bet

A come-out roll of a 7 or 11 is an automatic loser, a 2 or 3 an automatic winner, while the 12 (in some casinos the 2 instead) is a tie - nobody wins. Once the point is established, don't pass bettors win by the seven being thrown before the point is repeated.

Once the point is established, only the 7 and the point are consequential rolls for the pass and don't pass bettors. Winning bets pay even-money. Don't pass bets are made by placing the wager in the area marked *Don't Pass.*

Come and Don't Come Bets

They work exactly like the pass and don't pass bets except that these bets can be made only *after* the come-out roll, when a point is already established. (Pass and don't pass bets can be made only on a *come-out roll.*) These bets are made by placing the wager in the area marked *Come* or *Don't Come.*

Come Bet

7 or 11 on the first throw is a winner, a 2, 3 or 12 is a loser. After, the come point must repeat before the 7 is thrown to win. Pays 1-1, even money.

Don't Come Bet

7 or 11 on the first throw is a loser, a 2 or 3 a winner, and 12 is a standoff. (In some casinos 2 is the standoff and 12 is the winner.) Once the come point is estab-

lished, 7 must be thrown before the come point repeats for a winner. Pays even money.

Free-Odds Bets

To make a free-odds bet, the player must already have placed a pass, don't pass, come or don't come wager. Free odds bets are so named because the casino enjoys no edge on them.

Free-Odds: Pass Line

Once the point is established, the pass line bettor is allowed to make an additional wager, called a **free-odds bet**, that his point will repeat before a 7 is thrown. He may bet up to the amount wagered on the pass line and does so by placing the chips behind his pass line wager.

On come points of 4 or 10, the casino will pay 2 to 1 on a free-odds win, on points of 5 or 9, it will pay 3 to 2 and on points of 6 or 8, it will pay 6 to 5.

Free Odds: Don't Pass Line

Works the other way. Free-odds bettors wager that the 7 will be thrown before the point repeats. Since the odds favor the bettor once the point is established, there being more ways to roll a 7 than any other number, the don't pass free-odds bettor must **lay odds**, that is, put more money on the free-odds bet than he will win.

The allowable free-odds bet is determined by the *pay-off*, not the original bet. The bettor is allowed to win only up to the amount bet on the don't pass line.

We'll assume a $10 don't pass bet, which means the player can win only up to $10 on the free odds bet. On points of 4 or 10, the player must lay $20 to win $10; on points 5 and 9, he must lay $15; and on points 6 and 8, he must lay $12 to win that $10.

To sum up, the player must give 1 to 2 odds on points of 4 and 10, 2 to 3 odds on points of 5 and 9, and 5 to 6 odds on points 6 and 8.

Don't pass free odds bets are made by placing the wager next to the don't pass wager in the don't pass box.

Free Odds: Come and Don't Come Bets

These bets work the same as the free odds on the pass (corresponds to the come bet) and don't pass line (corresponds to the don't come) except they can only be made *after* the come point is established.

The only other difference is that the free-odds bet is not in play on the come-out roll, though the come bet itself is. (The free odds on the don't come, pass and don't pass bets are always in play.)

You make these wagers by giving your chips to the dealer - they'll place the bets for you.

Double Odds

Some casinos offer double odds as an inducement to the bettor. These work just like the odds bets described above except that even more money can be bet on the free odds wager. In the case of double odds, double the money could be wagered on the bet.

Place Bets

These are bets that a particular point number, the 4, 5, 6, 8, 9 or 10, whichever is bet on, will be rolled before a 7 is thrown. The player can make as many place bets as he wants. Place bets of 4 or 10 are paid at 9 to 5, on 5 or 9 are paid at 7 to 5 and 6 or 8 are paid at 6 to 5. These bets are not in play on the come-out roll.

Big 6 and Big 8

These are bets that the 6 (Big 6) or 8 (Big 8) are rolled before the 7. Winning bets are paid off at even money.

Field Bet

This is a one roll bet that the next roll of the dice will be a number listed in the field box - a 2, 3, 4, 9, 10, 11 or 12. Rolls of 2 and 12 pay double, all others in the box pay even money. Rolls of 5, 6, 7 and 8 are losers. This bet can be made anytime. (In some casinos, the 2 or 12 may pay triple.)

ONE ROLL BETS

These bets are about the worst you can find in a casino. They're found in the center of the layout and are made by giving the chips to the dealer.

The **Any 7** is a bet that the following roll will be a 7 and pays the winner 4 to 1; **Any Craps** is a bet that the following roll will be a 2, 3 or 12, pays 7 to 1; **2 or 12** is a bet that the next roll will be a 2 (or 12). You can bet either or both, pays 30 to 1. **3 or 11** is a bet that the 3 or the 11, whichever is chosen, will come up next. Pays 15-1.

The **Horn Bet** is a four-way bet that the next roll will be a 2, 3, 11 or 12. Pays off 15-1 on the 3 or 11 and 30-1 on the 2 or 12. The other three losing chips are deducted from the payoff.

Whenever the numbers 4, 6, 8 and 10 are rolled as doubles, the roll is said to be thrown **hardways**. Betting *hardways* is a wager that the doubled number chosen comes up before a 7 is thrown, or before the number is thrown *easy* (not as a double). Bets on hardways 6 or 8 pay 9 to 1, and on hardways 4 or 10, pay 7 to 1.

Right and Wrong Betting

Betting with the dice, pass line and come betting, is called *right betting*, while betting against the dice, making don't pass and don't come bets, is called *wrong betting*.

Betting right or wrong are equally valid methods of winning, with equivalent odds, and the choosing of either way, or alternating between the two, is merely a matter of personal style.

Winning Strategy

There are many bets available to the craps player, but to get the best chances of beating the casino, you must make only the bets which give the casino the least possible edge.

You can see from the chart that bets vary in house edge from the combined pass line: double odds wager where the house has but a 0.6% edge to the horn bet where the house edge can be as high as 16.67%!

To win at craps, make only pass and come bets backed up by free-odds wagers or don't pass and don't come bets, and back these wagers up with free-odds bets.

These bets reduce the house edge to the absolute minimum, a mere 0.8% in a single odds game or 0.6% in a double odds game if this strategy is followed.

By concentrating our bets this way, we're making only the best bets available at craps, and in fact, will place the majority of our bets on wagers the casino has absolutely no edge on whatsoever! This is the best way to give yourself every chance of beating the casino when the dice are hot and you've got bets riding on winners.

Try to keep two or three points going at one time by making pass and come bets if you're a right bettor, or don't pass and don't come bets if you're a wrong bettor and back all these bets with the full free odds available.

Money management is very important in craps, for money can be won or lost rapidly. However, try to catch that one good hot streak, and if you do, make sure you walk away a winner.

HOUSE EDGE IN CRAPS CHART

Bet	Payoff	House Edge
Pass or Come	1 to 1	1.41%
Don't Pass, Don't Come	1 to 1	1.40%
Free Odds Bets*	***	0.00%
Single Odds**	***	0.8%
Double Odds**	***	0.6%
Place 4 or 10	9 to 5	6.67%
Place 5 or 9	7 to 5	4.00%
Place 6 or 8	7 to 6	1.52%
Field	2 to 1 on 12	
	1 to 1 other #s	5.56%
Field	3 to 1 on 12	
	1 to 1 other #s	2.78%
Any Craps	7 to 1	11.11%
Any 7	4 to 1	16.67%
2 or 12	30 for 1	16.67%
	30 to 1	13.89%
3 or 11	15 for 1	16.67%
	15 to 1	11.11%
Hardways 4 or 10	8 for 1	11.11%
6 or 8	10 for 1	9.09%

*The free odds bet by itself
**The free odds bet combined with pass, don't pass, come and don't come wagers
***The payoffs on the free odds portion of the bets vary. See discussion under free odds for payoffs.

SLOTS

The allure of slot machine play has hooked millions of players looking to reap the rewards of a big jackpot!

There are basically two types of slot machines. The first type, the **Straight Slots**, pays winning combinations according to the schedule listed on the machine itself. These payoffs never vary.

The second type of machines are called **Progressive Slots.** These too have a standard set of payoffs listed on the machine itself, but in addition, and what sometimes makes for exciting play, is the big jackpot which progressively gets larger and larger, as every coin is put in. The jackpot total is posted above the machine and can accumulate to enormous sums of money!

The Basics

Slots are easy to play. Machines generally take anywhere from 1 to 5 coins, and all one needs to do is insert the coins into the machine, pull the handle and see what Lady Luck brings.

There are many types of slot machine configurations but all work according to the same principle - put the money in the slots and pull!

For example, some machines will pay just the middle horizontal line, while others may pay on any winning combination not only left to right, but diagonally as well. Other combinations exist as well.

Often, the number of lines the machine will pay on depends on the amount deposited. One coin only may pay the middle line, a second coin will pay the top line as well, a third coin - the bottom line, a fourth - the diagonal and a fifth - the other diagonal.

More winning rows do not necessarily equate to better

odds of winning. The odds are built into the machine and no amount of lines played will change them. The most important factor is how loose or tight the machines are set by the casino - that is what determines the odds facing a slots player.

Your best method is simply to play the machine most suited to your personal style.

Winning Strategy

The most important concept in slots is to locate the machines with the loosest setting, or with progressive machines, to play only the machines with the highest jackpot.

Some casinos advertise slots with returns as high as 97% to the player, others, even as high as 99%! Obviously, the player stands a much better chance of winning at these places than others where a standard return of only 84% might be the norm. On some machines, players may not even get an 84% return.

In general, the poorer paying machines will be located in areas where the casino or slots proprietor hopes to grab a few of the bettor's coins as he passes through an area or waits on a line.

Airport terminals, restaurant and show lines, bathrooms and the like tend to have smaller returns.

On the other hand, casinos that specialize in slots and serious slots areas within a casino will have better payoffs. These casinos view slots as an important income, and in order to keep regular slots customers, these bettors must hear those jackpot bells ringing - after all, winning is contagious!

Some machines are set to pay better than others, and these slots will be mixed in with poorer paying ones, so it's always a good idea to look for the hot machine. Better yet, ask the change girls. They spend all day near the slots and know which machines tend to return the most money. When you hit a jackpot, don't give the money back - make sure you walk away a winner!

SLOT CITY

Slots are huge money-makers for the casinos. On average, the typical Vegas slot machine pulls in more than $100,000 a year. At The Mirage, one cushy slot area allows you the pleasure of plunking $100 tokens into the one-armed bandits. And if that's too puny, several machines let you deposit $500 a throw!

With advances in computer technology, many slot machines have gone electronic. You can now push a spin button instead of pulling the lever. And many of the machines are tied together either in citywide or statewide networks, so the jackpots keep growing and growing.

*Operated by IGT (International Game Technology), five networks are now in operation. **Nevada Nickels Network** requires three nickels to win a statewide jackpot; **Quartermania** requires two quarters to win; **Fabulous Fifties** requires two half-dollar coins to win; **High Rollers** demands two $5 tokens to win big; and the most widespread of the networks, **Megabucks**, mandates a wager of three silver dollars to hit the huge enchilada. Megabucks jackpots start at $2 million. The record so far is held by a visiting nurse from California who took home $9.3 mil!*

In case you were planning on winning one of the outsized slots jackpots, casinos pay off over time in regular payments. But several casinos now pay some jackpots on the spot: the Boyd Group, operator of the California, Sam's Town, Fremont, and Stardust, offers a 25¢ slots network paying out $250,000 jackpots immediately. And Circus Circus's seven casinos in the state pay out $500,000!

KENO

There are 80 numbered squares on a keno ticket which correspond exactly to the 80 numbered balls in the keno cage. A player may choose anywhere from one number to fifteen numbers to play, and does so by marking an "x" on the keno ticket for each number or numbers he or she s chooses.

The Basics

Twenty balls will be drawn each game, and will appear as lighted numbers on the keno screens. Winnings are determined by consulting the payoff chart each casino provides. If enough numbers are correctly **caught**, you have a winner, and the chart will show the payoff. The more numbers caught, the greater the winnings.

Bets are usually made in .70 or $1.00 multiples, though other standard bets may apply, and a player may bet as many multiples of this bet as he desires as long as the bet is within the casino limits.

Marking the Ticket

The amount being wagered on a game should be placed in the box marked *Mark Price Here* in the upper right hand corner of the ticket.

Leave out dollar or cents signs though. $1 would be indicated by simply writing 1- and 70 cents by .70. Of course, any amount up the house limit can be wagered. Underneath this box is a column of white space. The number of spots selected for the game is put here. If six spots were selected on the ticket, mark the number 6, if fifteen numbers, mark 15.

This type of ticket, which is the most common one bet, is called a **straight ticket.**

5 SPOT STRAIGHT TICKET

MARK PRICE HERE

1	2	3	4	✗	6	7	8	9	10
11 ✗		13	14	15	16	17	18	19	20
21	22	23	24	25	26	27	✗	29	30
31	32	33	34	35	36	37	38	39	40

KENO LIMIT $50,000.00 TO AGGREGATE PLAYERS EACH GAME

41	42	43	44	45	46	47	48	49	50
51	52	53	54	✗	56	57	58	59	60
61 ✗		63	64	65	66	67	68	69	70
71	72	73	74	75	76	77	78	79	80

KENO RUNNERS ARE AVAILABLE FOR YOUR CONVENIENCE
WE ARE NOT RESPONSIBLE IF TICKETS ARE TOO LATE FOR CURRENT GAME

Split Tickets

A player may also play as many combinations as he chooses. **Split tickets** allow a player to bet two or more combinations in one game. This is done by marking two sets (or more) of from 1-15 numbers on a ticket and separating them by either a line, or by circling the separate groups. Numbers may not be duplicated between the two sets.

On split tickets in which several games are being played in one, the keno ticket should be marked as follows. In addition to the x's indicating the numbers, and the lines or circles showing the groups, the ticket should clearly indicate the number of games being played.

For example, a split ticket playing two groups of six spots each would be marked 2/6 in the column of white space. The 2 shows that two combinations are being played, and the 6 shows that six numbers are being chosen per game. If $1 is being bet per combination, we would put a 1- and circle it underneath the slashed numbers to show this, and in the *Mark Price Here* box, we would enter 2, to show $2 is being bet - $1 per combo.

Winning Strategy

Keno is a game that should not be played seriously, for the odds are prohibitively against the player. The house edge is typically well over 20% and higher - daunting odds if one wants to win in the long run.

One thing to look out for is that some casinos offer better payoffs on the big win than others, so a little shopping might get you closer to a bigger payoff. For example, some casinos will pay $50,000 if you catch all the numbers while another may pay just $25,000. Why not play for the $50,000?

Keno is a great game to test out your lucky numbers. Picking birth dates, anniversaries, license plate numbers, and the like offer a big pool of possibilities to see which ones will really pay off. If you know your lucky numbers, you may just give them a whirl and see if you can't walk away with a $50,000 bonanza!

POKER

Poker is played with a 52 card deck and can support anywhere from two to usually a maximum of about eight or nine players. There are many variations of this great game, the most popular being seven card high stud, high-low stud, lowball: draw poker, seven card stud, hold'em, and of course, jacks or better, and anything opens.

Let's go over the ranks of the hands in ascending

order, from the lowest ranking to the highest. We'll employ the following commonly used symbols: ace = A, king = K, queen = Q, Jack = J, and all others by their numerical symbol, such as nine = 9 and so on.

RANKS OF POKER HANDS

One Pair - Two cards of equal value, such as 7-7 or K-K.
Two Pair - Two sets of paired cards, such as 3-3 and 10-10.
Three of a Kind - Three cards of equal value, such as 9-9-9.
Straight - Five cards in numerical sequence, such as 3-4-5-6-7 or 10-J-Q-K-A.
Flush - Any five cards of the same suit, such as five hearts.
Full House - Three of a kind and a pair, such as 2-2-2-J-J.
Four of a kind - Four cards of equal value, such as K-K-K-K.
Straight Flush - A straight all in the same suit, such as 7-8-9-10-J, all in spades.
Royal Flush - 10-J-Q-K-A, all in the same suit.

Low Poker Rankings

In low poker, the ranking of hands are the opposite to that of high poker, with the lowest hand being the most powerful. The ace is considered the lowest and therefore the most powerful card, with the hand 5 4 3 2 A being the best low total possible.

Play of the Game

Many games use a **blind**, a mandatory bet that must be made by the first player to act in the opening round of play, regardless of cards. Some games require an **ante,** a uniform bet placed by all players into the pot before the cards are dealt.

Except for the times when a bet is mandatory, as is usually the case in the initial round of play, the first player to act in a betting round has three options: He can **bet** and does so by placing money in the pot, he can **check** or **pass**, make no bet at all and pass play on to the next player; or he can **fold** or **go out**, throw away his cards and forfeit play in the hand.

Once a bet is placed, a player no longer has the option of checking his turn. To remain an active player, he must either **call the bet**, place an amount of money into the pot equal to the bet; or he can **raise (call and raise)**, call the bet and make an additional bet.

If a player doesn't want to call the bets and raises that have preceded him, then he must fold and go out of play. Each succeeding player, clockwise and in turn, is faced with the same options: calling, folding or raising.

When play swings around to the original bettor, he or she must call any previous raises to continue as an active player as must any subsequent players who have raises due, or he must fold. A player may raise again if the raise limit has not been reached.

The number of raises permitted vary with the game, but generally, casino games limit the raises to three or five total in any one round, except when only two players are left, when unlimited raising is allowed. A player may only raise another player's bet or raise, not his own bet.

Play continues until the last bet or raise is called by all active players, and no more bets or raises are due any player. The betting round is now completed and over.

Check and raise, a player's raising of a bet after already checking in a round, is usually allowed.

Betting Limits (Limit Poker)

Betting in poker is often structured in a two-tiered level, such as $1-$2, $1-$3, $5-$10, $10-$20 and $30-$60.

When the lower limit of betting is in effect, for example in a $5-$10 game, all bets and raises must be in $5 increments, and when the upper range is in effect, all bets and raises must be in $10 increments. We'll show when these are in effect for the individual games.

Table stakes is the rule in casino poker games, and states that a player's bet or call of a bet may not exceed the amount of money he has in front of him.

A *tapped-out* player can still receive cards until the showdown and play for the original pot, but can no longer take part in the betting, and has no part in the **side pot** in which all future monies in this hand are placed by the active remaining players.

The **showdown** is the final act in a poker game, after all betting rounds are concluded, where remaining players reveal their hands to determine the winner of the pot. The player with the best hand at the showdown wins all the money in the pot, or in the unlikely event of a tie, then the pot is split evenly among the winners.

If only one player remains in the game at any time, there is no showdown and the remaining player automatically collects the pot.

The biggest difference between casino poker and private poker games is that the dealer in a casino game is not a player as he would be in a private game, and that the casino dealer receives a **rake**, a small cut of the action for his services.

Understanding the Rules of the Game

Though poker is basically the same game played anywhere, rules vary from game to game. Before playing, know the answers to the following questions:

    1. What are the betting limits?

2. Is "check and raise" allowed?

3. Are antes and blinds used, and if so, how much?

4. What are the maximum number of raises allowed?

5. When playing a casino game, the additional question, "How much is the rake? should be asked.

Draw Poker Variations

All bets before the draw in draw poker games, high or low, are in the lower tier of the betting limits when a two-tiered structure such as $1-$2 or $5-$10 are being used, and in the upper limit after the draw is completed.

Draw Poker: Jacks or Better

Each player is dealt five cards face down, and their identity is known only to him. There are two betting rounds. The first occurs before the **draw**, when players have an opportunity to exchange up to three unwanted cards for new ones, or up to four cards, if the remaining card is an ace. (Casinos allow players to exchange all five cards if desired.)

The draw occurs after the first betting round is completed with each remaining player, proceeding clockwise, drawing in turn. The second round of betting follows the draw, and once completed, the showdown occurs.

Draw Poker: Anything Opens

This variation is played exactly the same as in jacks or better except that any hand, regardless of the strength, may open the betting.

Lowball: Draw Poker

In this game, the lowest hand wins. The ace being the lowest value is the best card, and the hand 5 4 3 2 A, called a **wheel** or **bicycle**, is the best hand.

In lowball, the high card counts in determining the value of a hand: the lower the high card, the better the hand. When the high cards of competing hands are equivalent, the next highest cards are matched up, and the lowest value of these matched cards determines the winner. The hand 8 6 4 3 2 is a stronger total than 8 7 3 2 A.

When competing hands are the same, the hand is a tie and the pot is split. Straights and flushes are not relevant in lowball and do not count.

Players may draw as many cards as they want at the draw, exchanging all five cards if so desired.

There are two betting rounds, one before the draw and one after, and then there is the showdown, where the lowest hand collects the plot.

Seven Card Stud Poker Variations

In each variation, players form their best five card combination out of the seven dealt to produce their best hand. In seven card high stud, the highest ranking hand remaining wins the pot. In seven card low, the lowest hand wins.

And in high-low stud, players vie for either the highest ranking or lowest ranking hands, with the best of each claiming half the pot.

In each variation, players receive three initial cards, two face down and one face up. This marks the beginning of the first betting round. The following three cards are dealt face up, one at a time, with a betting round accompanying each card. The last card, the seventh, comes *down and dirty*, and is the third and last closed card received by the players.

At the showdown, remaining players now hold three

hole cards (hidden from the other players view) and four open cards. These are their final cards. One more round of betting ensues and then the showdown occurs.

Hold 'Em

This is the game best associated with free-wheeling poker. Players receive two downcards and combine these with five face-up community cards pooled in the middle to form their best five card hand.

Altogether, hold 'em has four betting rounds, beginning with the initial deal where all players receive two face down hole cards. The player to the left of the dealer must make a mandatory opening bet in the opening round. Subsequent players must either call (or raise) to play, or they must fold.

Once the initial betting round is over, it is time for the flop. Three cards are turned face up in the center of the table and this is followed by the second round of betting.

Two more open cards, one at a time, will be dealt face up in the center of the table, with a round of betting following each, and then the showdown where the highest ranking hand wins, or if all opponents have folded, then the last remaining player takes the pot.

BACCARAT

Baccarat is a game that combines the allure and glamour of European tradition with relatively low house odds, 1.17% betting Banker and 1.36% betting Player.

However, baccarat can be played by anyone. There's no need to bet mini-fortunes or even to play at high stakes. It is a leisurely game, and there are no decisions to make except for how much you want to bet and which position, Player or Banker, you decide to wager.

If you're still intimidated by the big tables, the mini-baccarat tables, now found in most casinos alongside the blackjack tables, can be a good place to begin play and become accustomed to the game.

The low casino edge makes baccarat a perfect place to try your favorite betting system, and at the same time, it's a game you can play in style!

The Basics of Play

Baccarat is a simple game to play even for beginners, for the **dealer** or **croupier**, directs all the action according to fixed rules.

Baccarat is played with from six to eight decks of cards dealt out of a shoe. Bets must be placed before the cards are dealt and are made by placing the chips in the appropriate box, **Banker** or **Player**, located in front of the bettor on the layout.

No matter how many players are betting in a game, only two hands will be dealt; one for the Banker position and one for the Player position.

Cards numbered 2 to 9 are counted according to their face value, a 2 equals 2 points, an Ace equals one point and a 7 equals 7 points. The 10, Jack, Queen and King have a value of 0 points and have no effect when adding up the points in a hand.

Points are counted by adding up the value of the cards. However, hands totaling 10 or more points, have the first digit dropped so that no hand contains a total of greater than 9 points. For example, two nines (18) is a hand of 8 points and a 7 5 (12) is a hand of 2 points.

The hand with the closest total to 9 is the winner, while the worst score is zero, called **baccarat.** A tie is a standoff or push, neither hand wins.

There are two opposing sides, the **Player** and the **Banker**, and initially, after the betting is done, each side will receive two cards. Bettors may wager on either hand.

A dealt total of 8 or 9 points is called a **natural**, and no additional cards will be drawn. It is an automatic win unless the opposing hand has a higher natural (a 9 vs. an 8), or the hand is a tie.

On all other totals, the drawing of an additional card depends strictly on established rules of play and will be handled by the croupier. There is never more than one card drawn to a hand in any case.

The Player's hand will be acted upon first, and then the Banker's.

Let's sum up the rules for drawing a third card or not in baccarat and than we'll show the rules in chart form for both the Banker and Player positions.

Situation 1 - Either the Player or the Banker position has a natural 8 or 9. It is an automatic win for the hand with the natural. If both hands are naturals, the higher natural wins. (A natural 9 beats a natural 8.)

If the naturals are equal, the hand is a tie.

Situation 2 - If the Player position has a 0-5, Player must draw another card; if a 6-7, the Player must stand.

Situation 3 - If Player stands, than the Banker hand follows the same rules as the Player position - it must draw on totals of 0-5 and stand on 6-7.

Situation 4 - If Player draws, Banker must draw or stand according to the value of the third card dealt as show below in the Banker Rules chart.

BANKER RULES		
Banker Two Card Total	Banker Draws When Giving Player This Card	Banker Stands When Giving Player This Card
0 - 2	0-9	
3	0-7, 9	8
4	2-7	0-1, 8-9
5	4-7	0-3, 8-9
6	6-7	0-5, 8-9
7	Banker Always Stands	
8-9	A Natural - Player Can't Draw	

Note that unless the Player has a Natural, the Banker always draws with a total of 0-2.

PLAYER RULES	
Two Card Total	Player's Action
0-5	Draw a Card
6 or 7	Stand
8 or 9	Natural. Banker cannot draw.

The winning hand in baccarat is paid at 1 to 1, **even money**, except in the case of the Banker's position where a 5% commission is charged on a winning hand. Commission is charged because of the inherent edge the Banker position has over the Player position.

With the commission, the Banker edge over the bettor is only 1.17%, quite low by casino standards. The house edge over the Player position is only slightly more, 1.36%.

During actual play, this commission is kept track of on the side by use of chips, and won bets at the Banker position are paid off at even money. This avoids the cumbersome 5% change-giving on every hand. The commission will be collected later; at the end of every shoe, and of course, before the player parts from the game.

Mini-Baccarat
This is the same game as regular baccarat except that it's played on a miniature blackjack-type table, and the bettors do not deal the cards.

ROULETTE

Roulette offers the player a multitude of possible bets, more than any other casino table game. All in all, there are over 150 possible combinations to bet. While roulette still gets some table action in Las Vegas, it is not nearly as popular as the single zero European game which offers the player much better odds than the American double zero game.

THE AMERICAN WHEEL

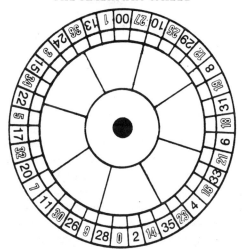

The Basics

Roulette is played with a circular wheel containing 36 numbers from 1 to 36 and a betting layout where players can place their wagers.

The Play of the Game

Play begins in roulette with the bettors placing their bets on the layout. The wheel will be spun by the dealer who will also throw the ball in the opposite direction from which the wheel is spinning. When the ball is about to leave the track, the dealer will announce that bets are no longer permitted.

When the ball has stopped in a slot, the outcome is announced, and the dealer settles won and lost bets.

Let's now look at the bets available at roulette.

THE BETS

Single Number Bet - A single number bet can be made on any number on the layout including the 0 and 00. To do so, place your chip within the lines of the number chosen, being careful not to touch the lines. Otherwise you may have another bet altogether. Payoff is 35 to 1.

Split Bet - Place the chip on the line adjoining two numbers. If either number comes up, the payoff is 17 to 1.

Trio Bet - The chip is placed on the outside vertical line alongside any line of numbers. If any of the three numbers chosen are hit, the payoff is 11 to 1.

4-Number Bet - Also called a **square** or **corner** bet. Place the chip on the spot marking the intersection of four numbers. If any come in, it is an 8-1 payoff.

5-Number Bet - Place the chip at the intersection of the 0, 00 and 2 to cover those numbers plus the 1 and 3. If any of these five land, the payoff is 6-1. It is the only bet not giving the house an edge of 5.26%. It's worse - 7.89%!

6-Number Bet - Also called a **block** bet. Wagers are placed on the outside intersecting line that separates the two sets of three numbers chosen. The payoff is 5-1.

Columns Bet - A chip placed at the head of a column, on the far side from the zero or zeros, covers all 12 numbers in the column and has a winning payoff of 2-1. The 0 and 00 are not included in this bet.

Dozens Bet - A bet on 1-12, 13-24 or 25-36. They're called the first, second and third dozen respectively. The winning payoff as in the column bet is 2 to 1.

THE EVEN MONEY BETS
You can also bet:

Red-Black - There are 18 black and eighteen red numbers. A player may bet either the red or the black and is paid off at 1 to 1 on a winning spin.

High-Low - Numbers 1-18 may be bet (low) or 19-36 (high). Bets are paid off at 1 to 1.

Odd-Even - There are 18 even numbers and 18 odd numbers. Winning bets are paid at 1 to 1.

THE ROULETTE LAYOUT

		0	00	
1to18	1st 12	1	2	3
		4	5	6
EVEN		7	8	9
		10	11	12
◇	2nd 12	13	14	15
		16	17	18
◆		19	20	21
		22	23	24
ODD	3rd 12	25	26	27
		28	29	30
19to36		31	32	33
		34	35	36
		2-1	2-1	2-1

Winning Strategy

First it must be stated clearly, that the casino has the mathematical edge over the player in roulette, and that no betting strategy or playing system can overcome those odds. Except for the five number bet which is at 7.89%, all bets at roulette give the house a 5.26% advantage.

You can have fun at roulette and come home a winner if you catch a good streak. Money management is all-important - protect your losses and quit when ahead. Betting strategies can work - in the short run - and provide the player with a fun, working approach to winning. And really, that's what the game is all about.

ROULETTE PAYOFF CHART		
Roulette Bets	**#**	**Payoff**
Single Number	1	35-1
Split Bet	2	17-1
Trio	3	11-1
4-Number (Corner)	4	8-1
5-Number	5	6-1
6-Number or Block	6	5-1
Columns Bet	12	2-1
Dozens Bet	12	2-1
Red or Black	18	1-1
High or Low	18	1-1
Odd or Even	18	1-1
# column is the amount of numbers covered by the bet.		

VIDEO POKER

This game is rapidly becoming the most popular machine game in the casinos. Decision-making and skill is involved, and proper play can make one a winner!

Video poker is basically played as draw poker. To play,

anywhere from one to five coins are inserted into the machine. Press the button marked ***DRAW/DEA***L (Sometimes the cards will be dealt automatically. In these cases there's no need to press the draw/deal button.)

The Draw/Deal Button

Five cards are dealt. The player may keep some or all the cards and does so by pressing the button marked hold underneath the corresponding card he wishes to keep. ***HELD*** will appear on the screen underneath each card or cards so chosen.

The DRAW/DEAL button is now pressed and those cards not chosen to be held will be replaced with new ones. This set of cards is the final hand.

A player may keep all five original cards and does so by pushing the hold button under each card; or he or she may discard all five original cards if so desired. This is done by pressing the DRAW/DEAL button without having pressed any of the hold buttons.

If your hand is a winner, the machine will flash "WINNER" at the bottom of the screen. Winning hands are automatically paid according to the payoffs shown on the machine.

Deuces Wild and Jokers Wild

Besides the Jacks or Better machine discussed above, some video poker machines are played as **deuces wild** or **jokers wild**. Wild cards can be given any value or suit and the machine will interpret wild cards in the most advantageous way for the player.

For example, the hand 2 2 5 6 8 in deuces wild would be a straight, for one 2 can be used as a 7 and the other as either a 9 or 4. The 2s could also be used as eights to give three of a kind, but since the straight is more valuable to the player the machine will see it as a straight.

Wild card machines have different payoff schedules than the jacks or better machines, and these payoffs will start giving credit only on a 3 of a kind hand or better.

Jacks or Better Payoffs

The following chart shows typical payoffs for video poker on a Jacks or Better machine. This machine is known as an **8-5 machine**, so named for the payoffs given on the full house and flush respectively.

PAYOFFS: JACKS OR BETTER: 8-5 MACHINE				
Coins Played	**1**	**2**	**3**	**4**	**5**
Jacks of Better	1	2	3	4	5
Two Pair	2	4	6	8	10
Three of a Kind	3	6	9	12	15
Straight	4	8	12	16	20
Flush	5	10	15	20	25
Full House	8	16	24	32	40
Four of a Kind	25	50	75	100	125
Straight Flush	50	100	150	200	250
Royal Flush	250	500	750	1000	4000

Progressives

Besides the straight machines discussed above, there are progressive machines, as in slots. All payoffs, like the straight machines, are fixed except in the case of a royal flush, where this grand-daddy pays the accumulated total posted above the machine on the electronic board.

This total slowly but constantly rises, and on a quarter machine in Las Vegas can rise into the thousands of dollars. Then the game gets more interesting!

WINNING HANDS IN VIDEO POKER

Jacks or Better - Two cards of equal value. Jacks or better refers to a pairing of Jacks, Queens, Kings or Aces.

Two Pair - Two sets of paired cards, such as 3-3 and 10-10.

Three of a Kind - Three cards of equal value, such as 9-9-9.

Straight - Five cards in numerical sequence, such as 3-4-5-6-7 or 10-J-Q-K-A.

Flush - Any five cards of the same suit, such as five hearts.

Full House - Three of a kind and a pair, such as 2-2-2-J-J.

Four of a kind - Four cards of equal value, such as K-K-K-K.

Straight Flush - A straight all in the same suit, such as 7-8-9-10-J, all in spades.

Royal Flush - 10-J-Q-K-A, all in the same suit.

Winning Strategy

The big payoff in video poker on the jacks or better machines is for the royal flush - a whopping 4,000 coins are paid for this score when five coins are played.

And on progressive machines, if a full five coins are played, the total could be a great deal higher, possibly as high as $3,000 (12,000 coins) on a quarter machine.

Of course, the royal doesn't come often. With correct strategy, you'll hit one every 30,000+ hands on the average. This doesn't mean, however, that you won't hit one in your very first hour of play!

But meanwhile, you'll be collecting other winners such as straights, full houses and the like, and with proper play, all in all, you can beat the video poker machines.

To collect the full payoff for a royal flush, proper play dictates that you always play the full five coins for each game. Of course, those that want to play less seriously can play any amount of coins from 1 to 5.

Following are the correct strategies for the 9-6 Flattops.

JACKS OR BETTER: 9-6 FLATTOP STRATEGY

1. Whenever you hold <u>four cards to a royal flush</u>, discard the fifth card, even if that card gives you a flush or pair.

2. Keep a <u>jacks or better pair</u> and any higher hand such as a three of a kind or straight over three to the royal. Play the <u>three to a royal</u> over any lesser hand such as a low pair or four flush.

3. With <u>two cards to a royal</u>, keep four straights, four flushes, and high pairs or better instead. Otherwise, go for the royal.

4. Never break up a <u>straight or flush</u>, unless a one card draw gives you a chance for the royal.

5. Keep <u>jacks or better</u> over a four straight or four flush.

6. Never break up a <u>four of a kind</u>, <u>full house</u>, <u>three of a kind</u> and <u>two pair</u> hands. The *rags*, worthless cards for the latter two hands, should be dropped on the draw.

7. The <u>jacks or better pair</u> is always kept, except when you have four cards to the straight or royal flush.

8. Keep <u>low pairs</u> over the four straight, but discard them in favor of the four flushes and three or four to a royal flush.

9. When dealt <u>unmade hands</u>, pre-draw hands with no payable combination of cards, save in order; four to a royal flush and straight flush, three to a royal flush, four flushes, four straights, three to a straight flush, two cards to the royal, two cards jack or higher and one card jack or higher.

10. Lacking any of the above, with no card jack or higher, discard all the cards and draw five fresh ones.

(These strategies are not applicable to the 8-5 Progressives. For full strategy charts for all video poker games including the Progressives, Jokers Wild, Deuces Wild and more, you may want to order the strategy in the back.)

8. THINGS TO DO - DAY AND NIGHT

Okay, so you've decided to come up for air from the murky depths of the casinos? Gamboling - well, how about promenading? - along the Strip or Downtown to see what's out there can be just as much fun as gambling, and will probably be easier on your wallet.

In this chapter we'll lay out the things to do in each part of town, during the day and into the late evening hours. We'll also show you the variety of Vegas entertainment options, from the big, flashy production shows and lizard lounge acts to the best places to go dancing and salooning.

There's a lot more going on in this town than most first-time visitors think. Las Vegas is home to several fine museums for both adults and children; beautiful parks where evening concerts are held under the summer moon; wacky water parks and miniature golf courses for family fun and games; and all sorts of local attractions, from the Liberace Museum to the Old Fort.

And Las Vegas' hotels are adding more theme parks, video arcades, and roller coaster rides all the time. Circus Circus' Grand Slam Canyon, MGM's Theme Park, and Mirage/Treasure Island's Pirates of the Caribbean are changing the face of the Vegas experience in ways we can only begin to guess at today.

DAYTIME ACTIVITIES

ALONG THE STRIP

DON PABLO CIGAR COMPANY

If you're a cigar fan, or just always wanted to see how the pros roll cigars the old-fashioned way, go to Don Pablo's at 3025 Las Vegas Blvd. S. (702/369-1818). The rollers are mostly Cuban, and if you've never seen one of these babies being rolled by an expert, you're in for a treat.

GUINNESS WORLD OF RECORDS MUSEUM

Located at 2780 Las Vegas Blvd. S. (702/792-3766) near Sahara Ave., the Guinness Museum features both Vegas and real-world feats, displayed through mock-ups, life-size dolls, photos, computers and TV screens. View the world's tallest man, the worlds' fattest man, the most tattooed woman in America, the world's biggest cat, and other record-breaking phenomena. See what some people will do to get their name into the record book.

OLD-TYME GAMBLING MUSEUM

Located at 3000 Las Vegas Blvd. S. (702/732-6111), the Old-Tyme Gambling Museum offers visitors a look at gambling artifacts through the ages, most from the early days of Nevada gaming. Even if you're not a big gambler, you'll find this place has some pretty cool stuff.

METZ PLAZA MUSEUMS

Three small museums opened in June 1993 at the **Metz Plaza**, located at 3765 Las Vegas Blvd. S. between the Aladdin and Tropicana hotels (702/798-3036). Each museum has a small gift shop attached. They are:

1) WORLD BOXING HALL OF CHAMPIONS

The firstMetz Plaza museum is worth visiting if you're a pugilist fan, with walls and walls of photos of great boxers through the years, in addition to championship belts and other boxing trophies.

"IRISH" JERRY QUARRY ON LIFE IN THE RING

Jerry Quarry was the winner of the 1965 Golden Gloves Award and contender for the world heavyweight championship. He fought twice with Muhammad Ali and twice with Joe Frazier. Quarry has taken to writing poetry and since Vegas is one of the premier boxing venues in the United States, we thought we'd share one of his poems with you:

*"I've been in the ring with the best of all men,
Some say the best of all time.
In boxing you're only as good as your last fight,
So you're only as good as your time.
In the ring with Frazier and Muhammad Ali
is a memory I look on with pride.
I fought with my heart but needed much more,
the bridesmaid but never the bride.
I look at my past, great memories abound,
for I fought, I bled, and I cried.
I gave my all round after round,
and the world knows and you know that I tried."*

Courtesy of "Irish" Jerry Quarry Promotions.

2) ELVIS, ELVIS, ELVIS

Elvis fans, you've found another treasure trove of Elvis mania. The museum features mementos from fans' personal collections, everything from photos, Elvis license plates, Elvis decanters, copies of the King's marriage certificate, and one of his black acoustic Fender guitars.

3) BETHANY'S CELEBRITY DOLL AND WAX MUSEUM

Dolls, dolls, and more dolls! That's what you'll find at Bethany's, celeb dolls of varying sizes, some life-size, some miniaturized, of famous Hollywood and political personages. The child in you (or your actual child if you're with one) will enjoy the first Barbie dolls, lifelike movie character and movie star dolls, and dolls from American history. A number of the likenesses are a bit of a stretch, but some are pretty good.

IMPERIAL PALACE AUTO COLLECTION

The Imperial Palace Hotel and Casino (3535 Las Vegas Blvd. S., 702/731-3311; admission) has over 200 antique and customized cars (motorcycles too) previously owned by the rich and famous. Some of the more notable automobiles are Hitler's custom-built Mercedes'; one of Mussolini's Alfa Romeo's; a 1913 Model T; a 1947 Tucker (only 51 were made); and several 1930's-era Caddies.

WET 'N WILD WATER PARK

Get soaked at Wet 'n Wild, 2601 Las Vegas Blvd. S. (702/737-3819), next to the Sahara Hotel. Swimming, floating, and sliding are all available here, in Wet 'N' Wild's 26 acres of pools, lagoons, and waterslides. More than 1.5 million gallons of water beckon you to get wet and act wild.

Park favorites include the Blue Niagara, a waterslide inside a 300-foot long blue loop; a wave-maker in the Wave Pool; the Black Hole water ride; and the new Bomb Bay, where you're dropped feet first from the Bomb Bay "capsule." Wet 'n Wild has become a Vegas institution, a great way to cool off in the blazing Nevada sun after a hard day at the buffet and gaming tables.

AROUND DOWNTOWN

Downtown is a much smaller area to cover, as noted at the beginning of this chapter. At night, just wandering into some of the more interesting casinos and hotels can be a lot of fun, particularly given all the big neon signs everywhere in the Glitter Gulch district. But there are some other places to hit as well.

We'll have more to say on the next few attractions in our **Kidstuff** chapter (Ch.13), but we'll list a few things here to do with your children in the greater Downtown neighborhood. The first three museums in particular seem to be favorites of the younger set.

LIED DISCOVERY CHILDREN'S MUSEUM

Kids love this place, located at 833 Las Vegas Blvd. N. (702/382-5437), an interactive facility with exhibits teaching children about science and life.

THE OLD FORT

Sometimes called The Old Mormon Fort (908 Las Vegas Blvd. N., 702/382-7198), the fort is the oldest surviving building in Nevada. The Old Fort will give you and your family an idea of what things were like when Las Vegas was first settled by Mormon settlers in 1855. The remaining fort is an adobe structure and has exhibits and artifacts from the early days. An archaeological dig is now in progress.

RIPLEY'S BELIEVE IT OR NOT MUSEUM

At the Four Queens Hotel (202 E. Fremont St., 702/385-4011; admission), Ripley's Believe It Or Not has some pretty cool exhibits. Robert Ripley was a newspaper columnist who asked us whether we believed it or not, and now there are a number of these museums around the country. Most of the usual oddball attractions found at other Ripley's Museums are here too - the torture chamber, various and sundry wax figurines, shrunken heads - with some Las Vegas-specific items, like the huge jelly bean roulette wheel.

LAS VEGAS NATURAL HISTORY MUSEUM

Located at 900 Las Vegas Blvd. N. (702/384-3466; admission), the museum is one of the better ones in the Southwest. They have one animated dinosaur, and they're building another. The fossil record comes alive here, extending from our Jurassic and Cretaceous friends (dinosaurs, that is) to today's animal kingdom.

LAS VEGAS LIBRARY

In the mood to read? Vegas doesn't have too many bookstores, but the Las Vegas Library (833 Las Vegas Blvd. N., 702/382-3493) is an award-winning building. The library looks like a kid's idea of a good time, which is always a good inducement to get the youngun's into a house of books. There's a good selection of local interest and local history books.

JOHNNY TOCCO'S RINGSIDE GYM

Watch heavyweights, welterweights, and lightweights

train at 9 W. Charleston Blvd. (702/387-9320). But you might want to refrain from commenting on their style or weak points. Let 'em find out in the ring!

FREMONT STREET EXPERIENCE

New developments are in store for Downtown. The Fremont Street Experience will be a $52 million latticed canopy covering Fremont Street from Main to Fourth Streets. Nightly laser shows and brightly-lit theme floats suspended from on high should liven things up a bit.

GREATER LAS VEGAS

Las Vegas has a fair number of museums and a growing number of art galleries and art boutiques. Most of them are located in the spreading vistas beyond the Strip. Like most other things about Vegas, the museums are mostly different fare than what you might be used to in other cities. We think they're pretty good, with one or two exceptions. We even learn a few things each time we go back to our favorite haunts.

LIBERACE MUSEUM

The most popular attraction in Las Vegas, bar none, is the Liberace Museum, located in - where else? - **The Liberace Plaza** at 1775 E. Tropicana Ave., 702/798-5595. Everything dear to "Mr. Showmanship," or Lee, as he was known to his close friends, is here. A native Wisconsonite, Liberace first started playing Vegas in 1942 and not long after made Vegas one of his homes.

The museum houses his outfits (what are today politically incorrect fox fur capes and coats, and sequined outfits of all sorts), his cars (including an incredible mirror-tiled

1962 Rolls Royce Phantom V Landau, one of seven made), his pianos (15 of them), his collections of antique desks, antique and miniature pianos (including a beautiful piano owned by Chopin), chandeliers, and rare musical instruments.

The world's largest rhinestone, valued at $50,000, is also on display. Unless you really despised the muzak of Liberace, you'll find the museum worth at least a brief stop. Proceeds from admission support The Liberace Foundation for the Performing and Creative Arts, which provides scholarships to "deserving and promising students."

If you're a Liberace fan, you'll be in Seventh Heaven. If you're not a fan, you may find the whole thing a bit of a "So What?" But what the heck, check it out.

LAS VEGAS ART MUSEUM

The Art Museum, located in **Lorenzi Park**, houses a relatively small permanent collection and rotating exhibits of (mostly area) artists' works for sale. The museum is located at 3333 W. Washington Blvd. 702/647-4300 (donations gratefully accepted).

CLARK COUNTY HERITAGE MUSEUM

Continuing with the museum thing, check out the Clark County Heritage Museum (1830 S. Boulder Highway, 702/455-7955; admission) en route to Hoover Dam. See the original Native American inhabitants of this region, and move on down through the ages to the first settlers (and the gambling artifacts they left behind), and the subsequent ghost towns that littered the landscape of the Old West after the frontier glory days.

The museum has a mining exhibit and a genuine 1905 Union Pacific steam engine, and a time-line exhibit showing

Nevada history through the ages. "Heritage Street" is where old houses and stores have been gathered from all over Southern Nevada and restored for your visiting pleasure. A recreated ghost town circa 1880 shows you what the place would have looked like back then, including mining equipment and pre-auto transportation.

NEVADA BANKING MUSEUM

Another museum that makes sense for Las Vegas, given how much money changes hands in this burg, is the Banking Museum (3800 Howard Hughes Parkway, 702/791-6223). Nineteenth-century American currency, old savings bonds, early gambling chips, antique teller machines and other relics from Nevada banking history are on exhibit here. A fun visit for history buffs and for those who can't get enough of the real thing.

MARJORIE BARRICK MUSEUM
OF NATURAL HISTORY

Las Vegas has not one but two natural history museums, the Las Vegas Natural History Museum mentioned earlier and the Marjorie Barrick Museum at the University of Nevada at Las Vegas (UNLV) campus (702/739-3381). A nice variety of living and extinct (and one near-extinct critter, the desert tortoise) flora and fauna can be found here. The most popular attraction here is the huge skeletal remains of the state fossil, the ichthyosaur - a marine dinosaur resembling a fish but far more dangerous in its day, which was about 100-150 million years ago!

NEVADA STATE MUSEUM
AND HISTORICAL SOCIETY

The State Museum (700 Twin Lakes Dr., 702/486-

5205; admission) has exhibits on early Native American social life, desert life, and Nevada history. We know you'll enjoy the nuke display (remember, not far away the Nevada Test Site is our nation's one and only nuclear weapons test facility). Public lectures, field trips, educational films and various workshops are also offered by the museum. Like the Las Vegas Art Museum, the Nevada State Museum is also on the grounds of **Lorenzi Park**.

SOUTHERN NEVADA ZOOLOGICAL PARK

Okay, enough museums. How about the zoo? While not terribly large, Nevada's only zoo is a great place to get some fresh air and see some wildlife. Located at 1775 N. Rancho Dr. (702/648-5955; admission fee), the zoo features the usual mix of animals from around the world and around the Southwest. The kids will like the petting zoo. One of the more interesting exhibits is the Bird Boutique, with many species of local and exotic birds.

NIGHTLIFE

THE STRIP

There is so much nightlife on or near the Strip that you shouldn't have any problem finding something fun to do. If you've come to gamble, you have your pick of the world's best casinos. The bigger theme hotels have movies, rides, circus acts, reasonably-priced restaurants, and of course many fine production shows.

If possible, try and purchase your tickets for the big shows (in particular, **Siegfried and Roy**, **Wayne Newton**, **The Splash Revue** or **Jubilee!**) before your arrival. Sold-out shows are not uncommon.

PROSTITUTION AND STRIP JOINTS

Prostitution is illegal in Clark County (Las Vegas), but it's not illegal just over the county line. A whole industry has sprung up outside of Las Vegas, which used to have a notorious prostitution scene. Nowadays, hawkers up and down the Strip or Downtown pass out leaflets for brothels, mostly in Nye County north of Las Vegas. With names like "Cherry Patch" and "Mabel's Whorehouse," these houses of ill-repute boast of the advantages of their legal status (weekly medical examinations, etc.). And, as you'll see from the flyers, these folks will send a limo to come and get you, while still other escort services will send girls directly to your room. They're easy!

If you want to look but not touch, you can visit the Can Can Room on Industrial Rd. off the Strip, the "World Famous Palomino" in North Vegas, or follow the ads on the back of taxicabs to the "Topless Girls of Glitter Gulch" Downtown. In addition to the Can Can, half-a-dozen or so strip joints have set up shop on Industrial Rd. behind the big hotels on the Strip.

PRODUCTION SHOWS, LOUNGE ACTS, AND COMICS

What are production shows? They're those big, flashy performances usually featuring some combination of dancing, singing, magic, comedians, acrobats, and anything else that dazzles the eye and mind.

We've listed only those current production shows scheduled for long-term runs. Virtually all hotels have lounge acts, whether they have big shows or not. And many comics either headline or perform in the smaller lounges.

Like most production shows, lounge acts change all the time, so check beforehand to see who's appearing.

The variety of shows on the Strip is a testament to the emphasis Vegas continues to place on big-name and big-value entertainment. *And away we go!!!!*

- **Aladdin**, 3667 Las Vegas Blvd. S., (702/736-0111; 800/634-3424). Aladdin Theater, Bagdad Showroom. Frequent comedy acts.
- **Arizona Charlie's**, 740 S. Decatur Blvd. (702/258-5200; 800/842-2695). Big Band dancing and topless shows at the Palace Grand Lounge.
- **Bally's**, 3645 Las Vegas Blvd. S. (702/739-4111; 800/634-3434). Jubilee Theater showing the **Jubilee!** show (watch the Titanic sink on stage); name acts in the Celebrity Room. Frequent comedy acts.
- **Bourbon Street**, 120 E. Flamingo (702/737-7200; 800/634-6956). Dixieland jazz bands in the main lounge.
- **Caesars Palace**, 3570 Las Vegas Blvd. S. (702/731-7110; 800/634-6001). Circus Maximus Showroom, lounge acts.
- **Circus Circus**, 2880 Las Vegas Blvd. S. (702/734-0410; 800/634-3450). Great circus acts (jugglers, trapeze artists, animal acts ... kids will love it) going on above casino in the Carnival Midway.
- **Continental**, 4100 Paradise Rd. (702/737-5555; 800/634-6641). Lounge acts.
- **Desert Inn**, 3145 Las Vegas Blvd. S. (702/733-4444; 800/634-6906). Crystal Room, Starlight Theater.
- **Excalibur**, 3850 Las Vegas Blvd. S. (702/597-7777; 800/937-7777). Medieval jousting and Merlin the Magician appear nightly in **King Arthur's Tournament** in King Arthur's Arena; lounge acts in other rooms.
- **Flamingo Hilton**, 3555 Las Vegas Blvd. S. (702/733-3111;

800/732-2111). Showroom features **City Lites** revue, with dancing, ice skating, and magic; name acts in Bugsy's Celebrity Theater.

· **Gold Coast**, 3120 Las Vegas Blvd. S. (702/367-7111; 800/331-5334). Dance Hall (biggest in state) featuring Country & Western music; lounge acts.

· **Hacienda**, 3950 Las Vegas Blvd. S. (702/739-8911; 800/634-6713). Showroom stars **Lance Burton: A Magical Journey,** and ice skating revues; lounge acts in Bolero Lounge.

· **Harrah's Las Vegas**, 3475 Las Vegas Blvd. S. (702/369-5000; 800/634-6765). Commander's Theater showing magic show **Spellbound - A Concert of Illusion;** also Claudine's Piano Bar and karaoke bar in the Court of Two Gators lounge.

· **Imperial Palace**, 3535 Las Vegas Blvd. S. (702/731-3311; 800/634-6441). Imperial Theater showing **Legends in Concert,** a rock impersonator show.

· **Las Vegas Hilton**, 3000 Paradise Rd. (702/732-5111; 800/732-7117). Showroom usually has big names, like Wayne Newton, Bill Cosby; Casino Lounge features the Jazz Barons and lesser-known acts.

· **Maxim**, 160 E. Flamingo Rd. (702/731-4300; 800/634-6987). Cabaret Showroom (comedians, singers), and Cloud Nine Lounge offering musical acts.

· **The Mirage**, 3400 Las Vegas Blvd. S. (702/791-7111; 800/456-7111). Theater Mirage Showroom features **Siegfried and Roy,** magic and wild animal show; **Cirque Du Soleil,** a circus show more for adults than kids; and various lounge acts in the Lagoon Saloon.

· **Palace Station,** 2411 W. Sahara Ave. (702/367-2411; 800/634-3101). Music in the Loading Dock Lounge.

· **Rio**, 3700 W. Flamingo (702/252-7777; 800/888-1808). Copacabana Showroom features **Brazilia,** music, dance, exotic tropical birds; Brazilian music in Mambo's Lounge.

- **Riviera**, 2901 Las Vegas Blvd. S. (702/734-5110; 800/ 634-6753). Versailles Theater shows **Splash,** where music and synchronized swimming meet in a 20,000 gallon water tank; Mardi Gras Lounge features **An Evening at La Cage** (female impersonators), plus music and topless dancing; Le Bistro Lounge. Comedy headliners.
- **Sahara**, 2535 Las Vegas Blvd. S. (702/737-2111; 800/634- 6411). Congo Theater features comedy acts and **Boylesque** (female impersonators) which may become a permanent fixture; musical acts in the Casbar Lounge.
- **San Remo**, 115 E. Tropicana Ave. (702/739-9000; 800/ 522-7366). Magic, comedy, singing in the Parisian Cabaret.
- **Sands**, 3355 Las Vegas Blvd. S. (702/733-5000; 800/446- 4678). Copa Room's current revue, **Bare Essence,** may become the headliner here, featuring topless dancers; Winners Circle has musical acts.
- **Showboat**, 2800 E. Fremont (702/385-9123; 800/826- 2800). Lounge acts.
- **Stardust**, 3000 Las Vegas Blvd. S. (702/732-6111; 800/ 634-6033). Stardust Theater showing **Enter the Night,** with music, dancing (some numbers topless), and the flying Vladimir; lounge acts in the Starlight lounge.
- **St. Tropez**, 455 E. Harmon St. (702/369-5400; 800/666- 5400). Lounge acts.
- **Tropicana**, 3801 Las Vegas Blvd. S. (702/739-2222; 800/ 634-4000). Tiffany Theater shows **Folies Bergere** Parisian dance and song revue (some topless numbers). Comedy Stop Room for comics, Atrium Lounge has music, and three free Island Laser Shows each night.
- **Vegas World**, 2000 Las Vegas Blvd. S. (702/382-2000; 800/634-6277). Galaxy Theater features comedians Allen & Rossi; musical acts in the lounge.

PIANO BARS

Not quite a lounge act, and certainly not a production show, music from the '30s a la Cole Porter, Rodgers and Hart, and Duke Ellington can be found outside the hotels at a cozy little piano bar called **Baby Grand**, 208 E. Sahara (702/791-0107).

Another nice, romantic piano bar is **Kiefer's Atop the Carriage House**, 105 E. Harmon (702/739-8000). Mostly jazz. The **Peppermill Inn**, 2985 Las Vegas Blvd. S. (702/735-7635), across from the Stardust Hotel, does not have live music, but does have a piano bar feel to it. There's a romantic and serene atmosphere here, a nifty trick for a bar on the Strip.

LET'S DANCE!

If you're a Country & Western (C&W) fan, you're in luck. One of the most fun and exciting dance halls in the state is the **Palladium,** at the corner of Industrial and Harmon Roads behind The Mirage and Caesars (3665 Industrial Rd; 702/733-6366; cover charge). Most of the dudes are wearing regulation Levi's and Stetson's, while most of the dudettes are also sporting cowboy hats and the kind of short skirts you see in ... well, in C&W places. The music is great and the dancing is mostly at the expert level.

One of the current hot clubs in Vegas is the **Shark Club**, 75 E. Harmon (702/795-7525), where hard rock is king. If you like it loud, you'll like it here. The fun takes place on three levels. The shark aquarium adds a touch of danger.

The Metz, right on the Strip at 3765 Las Vegas Blvd. S. (702/739-8855), in a shopping center by the same name, is another hard-rockin', dark, somewhat small place, but a good spot for beer guzzling (in moderation, of course) and dancing.

MOVIES ... SORT OF

Two movie theaters in town are unique. Check the local newspaper listings if you want to take in a movie at any one of Vegas's cinemas, but that's not what we want you to do; we want you to visit the two unique cinematic experiences below:

OMNIMAX THEATER

Part of **Caesars Palace**, 3570 Las Vegas Blvd. S. (702/731-7110; 800/634-6661), the Omnimax is easily spotted from the Strip, as laser lights flash on the outside of the geodesic dome-shaped theater. There's a self-parking lot for the theater out in front.

The extra-large screen format is perfect for viewing special films designed to take advantage of IMAX film technology and the Sensaround sound system. Your seats tilt at a 27-degree angle. Brilliant colors flash all around you. How much more could you want? The usual shows include special films that take you into space, through the air, and under the ocean. The big IMAX movies play here, like "Fires of Kuwait" and "To Fly."

MAGIC MOTION MACHINES

Further south along the Strip, **Excalibur** (3850 Las Vegas Blvd. S.; 702/597-7777) has two dynamic motion simulators, otherwise known as Magic Motion Machines. The theater is small, with six rows. A bar descends for you to rest your arms on, and the hydraulic pumps below do their work. You jiggle up, down, and sideways, while the action on the screen unfolds.

There are six very short three-minute films from which to choose: Devil's Mine Ride (the one to see if your time is short), Runaway Train, Desert Duel, Colossus Roller coaster, Ninja Roller coaster, and Revelation Roller coaster. The rides are even better than your average roller coaster ride, because you actually see your doom rising to meet you in beautiful panoramic color.

The **MGM Grand**, opening in February 1994, will also have a motion machine.

DOWNTOWN

There's not as much to do at night Downtown as on the Strip, but there are a small number of high-quality, popular extravaganzas and lounge acts.

PRODUCTION SHOWS, LOUNGE ACTS, AND COMICS

- **The California**, 12 Ogden Ave. (702/385-1222; 800/634-6255). Lounge acts in the Redwood Bar & Grill.
- **Fitzgerald's**, 301 E. Fremont (702/388-2400; 800/274-5825). Lounge acts in Main Casino.
- **Four Queens**, 202 E. Fremont (702/385-4011; 800/634-6045). Jazz acts Monday nights in the French Quarter Lounge; other musical acts during the week.
- **Golden Nugget**, 129 E. Fremont (702/385-7111; 800/634-3403). Revues and music in The Lounge.
- **Lady Luck**, 206 N. 3rd St. (702/477-3000; 800/523-9582). Showroom features **Melinda: The First Lady of Magic and Her Follies Revue.**

ROSIE O'GRADY'S GOOD TIME EMPORIUM

Neither a production show, nor a lounge act, nor a regular bar, at least as these things are commonly understood in Vegas, an amusing time can be had at **Rosie O'Grady's Good Time Emporium** (300 N. Main St. part of Main Street Station, 702/387-1896). New Orleans theme.

The good time at Rosie O'Grady's is helped along by a great Dixieland jazz band, waitresses who double as dancers, and a barkeep who knows how to mix drinks.

BARS AND SALOONS

- **Down Under Grill & Pub**, 300 S. Fourth St. (702/382-6162).   Decent food (but, interestingly enough, not Aussie as the name implies) and drinks.
- **Skyeroom**, at **Binion's Horseshoe Hotel**, 128 Fremont (702/382-1600). Come for a drink and the great view.

GREATER LAS VEGAS

As with restaurants, there is less selection, but there are some quality places off the beaten tourist path worth checking out. There are no big production shows out here, but there's good music, dancing and bars worth hitting.

LOUNGE ACTS

Many of the hotels in Greater Las Vegas have some form of entertainment, but no production shows to speak of. Remember, most of the hotels in greater Vegas are smaller, and acts here are limited to bar and lounge acts.

Two of the better lounges are at:
- **Sam's Town**, 5111 Boulder Highway (702/456-7777; 800/634-6371). Music at the Roxy Saloon.
- **Santa Fe**, 4949 N. Rancho Dr. (702/658-4900; 800/872-6823). Music (rock, jazz) and karaoke at the Ice Lounge.

DANCING AND LIVE MUSIC

- **Carollo's**, 2301 E. Sunset Rd. (702/361-3712).   Rock bands, good-sized dance space.
- **Calamity Jayne's**, 3015 Boulder Highway (702/384-4591). Hard, loud rock music; local and big-name bands.

- **501 Club**, 2585 E. Flamingo Rd. (702/732-0501). Rock bands playing Big Chill-era tunes. Two happy hours (one after midnight)!
- **The Hop**, 1650 E. Tropicana (702/736-2020). Hark back to the nostalgic days of yore ... not at Excalibur, good knight or lady, but at this fifties dance hall. Slick back your hair and get down to the music of Elvis, Fats Domino, your Motown favorites and lots more.
- **Play It Again, Sam**, 4120 Spring Mt. Rd. (702/876-1550). Jazz, blues acts. Good place to take a date (or even your spousal attachment).
- **Sam's Town Western Dance Hall**, 5111 Boulder Highway (702/456-7777; 800/634-6371). Great C&W dancing at a fun place.

BARS AND SALOONs

- **Arubas Lounge**, 1487 E. Flamingo (702/737-0727). Piano bar.
- **Cafe Michelle**, 1350 E. Flamingo (702/732-8687). Piano bar, lunch and dinner available. Good spot for outdoor patio dining.
- **Elephant Bar**, 2797 Maryland Pkwy (702/737-1586). You won't need your elephant gun here to hunt for big game (as in there's a big singles scene, so go forth and pick up).
- **Ferdinand's**, 5006 S. Maryland Pkwy (702/798-6962). On the gritty side, but fun. C&W music, pool table.
- **Shenanigan's**, 6145 W. Sahara (702/364-2535). Fancy mod nightclub, pool tables, games.
- **Sneakers**, 2250 E. Tropicana (702/798-0272). Sports bar with big-screen TV's.
- **Tommy Rocker's**, 3550 S. Decatur (702/368-7625). Good ol' fashioned rock 'n roll bar (restaurant attached).

9. SHOPPING

Who comes to Las Vegas to shop? Nobody. But Las Vegas does offer a lot of shopping choices, and those choices keep getting better. The stores and the layout in **Caesars Forum** have got to be seen to be believed, while the **Fashion Show Mall** and the **Boulevard Mall** also have fancy shopping but offer a greater variety of more affordable stores. And there's good discount shopping at the **Las Vegas Factory Stores** south of the Strip.

At all of these malls, clothes, jewelry, and shoes seem to be the main event, but you can also find a good selection of gifts and souvenirs.

There is less diversity Downtown, although there are some nice Indian jewelry shops. Not far from Downtown, you'll find some interesting antique stores, but not too much of anything else. Outside both main tourist areas you'll find more run-of-the-mill mall shopping.

The bigger hotel/casinos tend to have more shops or shopping arcades than the smaller hotels that have one or two stores or a basic ticky-tacky gift shop.

THE STRIP

CAESARS FORUM

You have to see this place to believe it! **Caesars Forum** and the **Appian Way** shops are both part of the most elaborate and upscale shopping extravaganza Vegas has ever seen. They're both part of **Caesar's Palace Hotel** at 3570 Las Vegas Blvd. S., 702/731-7110.

Caesars Forum is the largest hotel mall in the city, with ninety stores offering mostly expensive shopping. The indoor mall is beautifully done, with tons of chic marble and a painted sky overhead that changes from day into night. The unique **Festival Fountain** features the four gods Bacchus, Apollo, Pluto, and Venus, who move, talk, and play the harp. Overhead, an amazing light show dances off the ceiling with interludes of lightning, thunderbolts, and images from Roman mythology. The fun begins every hour on the hour, from 10:00 am to 10:00 pm.

Some of the exclusive clothing and jewelry stores you'll find at Caesars Forum are **Gucci's**, **Cartier's**, **Versace**, **Bernini Donna** and **Vasari**. If you're into cool ties, check out **The Tie Knot** (Kranmar bought himself two wild beauties here). For elegant shoes, try **Avventura** or **Bruno Magli**. There are eleven restaurants, including the famous LA hot spot, **Spago**.

BALLY ARCADE

The attractive shopping arcade in **Bally's Hotel** (3645 Las Vegas Blvd. S., 702/739-4111) is the second-largest hotel shopping mall, with more than 40 shops. Stores here, featuring the likes of **Mort Wallin** for men and **Marshall-Rousso** for women, sell fancy duds, shoes and furs, jewelry, gifts, Asian and American Indian arts and crafts, and more. Both malls have delicious chocolate and candy shops.

FASHION SHOW MALL

One of the nicest malls in town, with nearly 150 stores, is located at 3200 Las Vegas Blvd. S., right next to the Mirage Hotel (702/369-8382). Here you'll find exclusive shopping in small boutiques, like **Uomo's** and **North Beach Leather**, and large department stores (**Saks**, **Nieman-Marcus**, and **Dillards).** There is a great selection of clothes and accessories here, particularly shoes and hats, and the Mall also has some very classy galleries.

SOUVENIR SHOPS

There are a jillion souvenir shops in every nook and cranny on the Strip; most seem to offer the same things at roughly the same prices. If don't mind giving someone something that could be perceived as tacky, any of these shops will do. The oft-visited and always crowded **Bonanza: World's Largest Gift Shop** across from the Sahara Hotel (2400 Las Vegas Blvd. S.; 702/384-0005) is one of the better choices, if for no other reason than its impressive choice of souvenirs and gifts.

DOWNTOWN

The Strip doesn't have all the good stores in this city. Downtown has some pretty good shopping too, particularly for Indian jewelry and antiques.

AMERICAN INDIAN JEWELRY

A number of American Indian stores are well worth visiting if you fancy Native Americana goods. Four of the best are:
• **Trader Bill's**, 324 Fremont St., 702/384-4408)
• **Turquoise Chief**, 1408 Las Vegas Blvd. S. (702/385-7011)
• **Desert Indian Shop**, 108 N. Third St. (702/384-4977)
• **Turquoise Chief**, 1334 Las Vegas Blvd. S. (702/383-6069).

ANTIQUE ROW

Not far from Downtown lies Vegas's antique row, although most stores are scattered over a fairly broad area. Many are located along **East Charleston Blvd.**, and they sell all manner of collectibles from all over the world, not just from Las Vegas's short but glorious past.

Three of the more interesting and fun antique stores are the **Sunshine Clock Shop** at 1651 E. Charleston (702/363-1312), which has a unique collection of European and American clocks, a number of which date from the 19th century; **Sweet D's**, 2014 E. Charleston (702/382-0933), featuring a great selection of antique radios and jukeboxes; and **Buzz & Co. Fine Antiques** at 2034 E. Charleston (702/384-2034), where the prices are high but the goods are the real thing, including well-preserved Tiffany lamps, 19th-century French and English furniture, and other fancy accoutrements.

GREATER LAS VEGAS

THE MEADOWS

The Meadows (4300 Meadows Ln., 702/878-3331), west of Downtown, has pretty much the same kinds of stores you'd find in any mall across America. The Meadows has about 150 stores plus four big department stores. As a rule, the stores are more reasonably priced than the exclusive mall stores along the Strip.

COMMERCIAL CENTER

The Commercial Center, at 953 E. Sahara Ave., has a decent number of shops but is best known for its Asian groceries, restaurants, and stores.

THE BOULEVARD MALL

The main shopping emporium in greater Vegas is situated on Maryland Parkway (3528 Maryland Parkway, 702/735-8268). The huge mall has less expensive stores than the malls on the Strip. The recently completed expansion has brought in dozens of new stores and the distinction of being the largest shopping complex in the state at 1.2 million square feet.

LAS VEGAS FACTORY STORES

Discount mania lives six miles south of Excalibur at 9115 Las Vegas Blvd. S. The Las Vegas Factory Stores offer more than 70 retail and outlet shops, including the likes of **Corning**, **Mikasa**, **Geoffrey Beene**, and **Adolfo II**. Savings are often 50 percent or more on many items. CAT bus service makes the trip once an hour; **take bus number 19** from the Strip.

ETHEL M CHOCOLATES

In Henderson, an outgrowth of Las Vegas not far from Downtown, you'll find one of Las Vegas's most popular attractions: Ethel M, 2 Cactus Garden Dr., Henderson (702/458-8864). You can take a free factory tour where the Mars family makes their chocolates - Mars Bars, M&M's, and other chocolate delectables beginning with the letter M. The factory and store are owned by the Mars chocolate empire, and only in Nevada can you get Mars chocolate snacks with alcohol! There's also a cactus garden adjoining the store that's worth strolling through.

THE GALLERIA MALL

Slated to open in Henderson in 1994, The Galleria will be a monstrous affair, rivaling The Boulevard Mall at 1.2

million square feet of shopping space. The big department stores will be Dillards, May Co., and Mervyn's.

UNUSUAL SHOPPING

Want to buy a neon sign? Who doesn't, right? Go to **Young Electric Sign Company (YESCO)** at 5119 Cameron St. (702/876-8080). With no traffic, it's only five minutes from the Strip, and a fun place to visit. Whether you're in the market to buy or just gaze, **Beck Neon** (3889 Spring Mountain Rd.; 702/362-0616) has some terrific neon art on display.

And what visit to any Western town would be complete without checking out the threads, boots, and Stetsons at a place like **Sam's Town Western Emporium**, 5111 Boulder Highway (702/454-8017) or **Adams Western Store**, 1415 Western Ave. (702/384-6077).

If you're looking for something different to bring home, visit the **House of Antiques and Slots**, located between the Strip and Downtown (1243 Las Vegas Blvd. S., 702/382-1520). You can buy old slot machines and other gambling goodies, like old chips and dice. Just off the Strip, you can buy the same stuff the casinos purchase at **Paul-Son Dice and Card** (2121 Industrial Rd., 702/384-2425).

And if you've ever had fantasies of dressing like a real-live dealer or croupier on Bingo Night back home, then a visit to the **Dealers Room Casino Clothiers**, 3661 Maryland Parkway S. (702/732-3932), is a must.

For more gambling goodies, the Downtown area offers two unique stores: The Gamblers Book Club and the Gamblers General Store.

GAMBLERS BOOK CLUB

The **Gambler's Book Club**, 630 S. 11th St. (702/382-

7555), serving gamblers who read since 1964, has the best and most extensive selection of gambling and gaming books in the country, including a large number dealing with Las Vegas gambling history and gambling anecdotes.

This book store is a tradition of sorts in Las Vegas - a must-see if you're a gambler. Ask Howard Schwartz or Edna Luckman (the owner) any question about gambling books or gambling arcana and they'll put you straight.

GAMBLERS GENERAL STORE

Nearby is the **Gamblers General Store** at 800 S. Main St. (702/382-9903), which offers much of the same plus antique slot machines, poker chips, roulette tables, and a good selection of other gambling necessities.

10. GOOD EATS

Las Vegas has a great variety of restaurants, from the mundane and monotonous to the sublime and superb. There are a lot of cheap restaurants, some serving food all night, and there is a good variety of culinary offerings from all over the world. That being said, with some notable exceptions, Vegas is not known for its gourmet dining, and quite often the low price matches the low quality. But for the money, you'll usually get good, solid food, and plenty of it.

There are bargains to be had, as well as fine meals, if you know where to go. Here are some of our favorites, organized by type of cuisine. As we have in other chapters, we've listed the city's restaurants by location (The Strip, Downtown, and Greater Las Vegas) and by price (Inexpensive, Moderate, Expensive).

The Strip has the best and most extensive restaurants, but there are many fine eateries beyond the big hotels on Las Vegas Blvd. South. The restaurant scene Downtown is much smaller, but there are a few winners. The **Golden Nugget**, for example, is a gold-mine of good restaurants, and if you only ate here while you were in town, you'd come away thinking Vegas was one hell of a great food town. Compared to the Strip, however, the choice is much smaller.

For most tourists, the restaurant selection outside the Strip and Downtown will probably seem somewhat remote.

There are not as many touristy places to eat - but it's also true that there are some real good dining establishments out here. With a small effort in most cases, you can find some relatively inexpensive choices, and you'll see the other Vegas up close and personal.

Here are our citywide picks, from the buffet tables to the more well-heeled eateries.

We give buffets their own category right up front, since they're the lifeblood of Las Vegas' dining scene. Any discussion of restaurants in this city would be incomplete without a few words on this great institution. Buffets are what Vegas is all about - visitors from all over the world paying a few bucks for a huge meal, after they've dropped a few hundred at the tables, and coming away convinced they just got a great deal! And if you go to the right buffet, you *will* get a great deal.

BUFFETS

A class unto itself in Las Vegas, most hotel buffets are inexpensive affairs, costing anywhere from $2-8, depending on whether you're having breakfast, lunch, or dinner, and what the food du jour happens to be.

These are our picks arranged by location:

THE STRIP

- **Aladdin** - They call their ethnic buffet "international;" bigger selection than the Flamingo buffet.
- **Bally's** - Sunday champagne brunch is excellent. Popular Vegas buffet.
- **Caesar's Palace** - Palatium Buffet overlooks an extensive sports betting operation that looks like NASA's Mission Control. Good turkey and salad bar. Fresh whipped

cream with your strawberries.

- **Excalibur** - Medieval theme at the "Round Table" is mostly fun for the kids; the carved roast beef and turkey are pretty good.
- **Flamingo Hilton** - Ethnic buffet is usually pretty good.
- **Frontier Hotel** - The Friday seafood buffet is justly famous. Shrimps galore!
- **Las Vegas Hilton** - Standard but good buffet fare.
- **Mirage -** Many consider this the best buffet in town, and we like it too! Many quality selections and impressive desert bar. Dine in colorful, yet classy setting.
- **Palace Station** - Inexpensive and solid, resident Vegans come here in droves.
- **Rio** - Chinese, Italian, Mexican, and other foods are adequate, but go straight to the Amazon Grill in the Carnival Buffet for tasty but pseudo-Brazilian fare.
- **Stardust** - Excellent selection. You'll enjoy this buffet.

DOWNTOWN

There are only two buffets we'd suggest in the Downtown area. Several other hotels offer buffets, but the results are not great. Stick with these two if you are having your chow Downtown:

- **Fremont** - Great deal for the money.
- **Golden Nugget** - Excellent food, good setting.

GREATER LAS VEGAS

There aren't too many quality buffets outside the Strip and Downtown, although a number of the smaller places do offer them. We'd recommend two along Boulder Highway:

- **Sam's Town** - Solid beffet, will get the job done.
- **Showboat -** Popular with locals, good food for the money.

STEAK AND PRIME RIB

Steak and roast beef were for a long time the staple of Vegas gamblers. Now, of course, there are many other foods to choose from, but for many visitors Las Vegas is still a place where you wash down your free drinks with a thick juicy steak or a tender prime rib.

We think these are the best of the lot, based on quality of food, service, and value for your hard-earned dollar. For those restaurants that are part of a hotel, the hotel name follows the listing and we include the phone number.

THE STRIP

Expensive
- **The Charcoal Room, The Hacienda Hotel** (702/739-8911)
- **The Flame**, 1 Desert Inn Rd. (702/735-4431)
- **Barrymores' Steak House, Bally's** (702/739-4111)
- **Claudine's**, **Harrah's Las Vegas Hotel** (702/369-5000)

Moderate
- **Wellington's Steak House, Aladdin** (702/736-0111)
- **Golden Steer**, 308 W. Sahara Ave. (702/384-4470)
- **Caravan Room, The Sahara Hotel** (702/737-2111)
- **William B's, The Stardust Hotel** (702/732-6111)
- **The Steak House, Circus Circus Hotel** (702/734-0410)

Inexpensive
- **Sir Galahad's, Excalibur Hotel** (702/597-7777)
- **Michelle's Cafe, The Frontier Hotel** (702/734-7110) Roast Beef specials.

DOWNTOWN

Expensive
- **Elaine's**, **Golden Nugget Hotel** (702/385-7111). Also serves other excellent beef dishes, seafood.

Moderate

- **Centerstage**, **Jackie Gaughan's Plaza Hotel** (702/386-2512). Best view of neon-lit Glitter Gulch if you get a window seat.
- **Redwood Bar and Grill, California Hotel** (702/385-1222).
- **Hugo's Cellar, Four Queens Hotel** (702/385-4011). Both steak and other meats are excellent.
- **Binion's Steak house, Binion's Horseshoe Hotel** (702/382-1600).

Inexpensive

- **The Prime Rib Room**, **Lady Luck Hotel** (702/477-3000).

GREATER LAS VEGAS

Moderate

- **Anthony's**, 3620 E. Flamingo 702/454-0000). Where else can you get lion, camel, and alligator steaks?
- **Bob Taylor's Ranch House**, Rio Vista St. at US-95 (702/645-1399).
- **Hard Rock Cafe**, 4475 Paradise Rd. (702/733-8400). Look for the huge Electric Guitar in front.
- **Mt. Charleston Restaurant**, Kyle Canyon in Mt. Charleston. Northwest of town (702/386-6899). Specialty is game.
- **The Tillerman**, 2245 E. Flamingo (702/731-4036). Steak and seafood.
- **Tommy's Barbecue**, 1505 E. Flamingo (702/734-1880). Like the name says, barbecue's the thing here.

Inexpensive

- **Gates**, 2710 E. Desert Inn Rd. (702/369-8010). Barbecue joint.

SEAFOOD

THE STRIP

Expensive
- **Kokomo's, Mirage Hotel** (702/791-7111). Seafood and steak.
- **Rosewood Grille**, 3339 Las Vegas Blvd. S. (702/792-9099). Lobster and steak specialties.

Moderate
- **Port Tack**, 3190 W. Sahara Ave. (702/873-3345)
- **Famous Pacific Fish Company**, 3925 Paradise Rd. (702/796-9676)

Inexpensive
- **Fisherman's Broiler**, The Palace Station Hotel (702/367-2411)

DOWNTOWN

Moderate
- **Rafters**, 1350 E. Tropicana (702/739-9463)

CONTINENTAL AND GOURMET

THE STRIP

Expensive
- **Bacchanal, Caesars Palace** (702/731-7731). Expensive. Roman toga party minus the togas.
- **Pegasus, Alexis Park** (702/796-3300)
- **Michael's, Barbary Coast Hotel** (702/737-7222)
- **Gigi, Bally's Hotel** (702/739-4111)
- **Bistro, Mirage Hotel** (702/791-7111). French.
- **Le Montrachet, Las Vegas Hilton** (702/732-5111). French.

DOWNTOWN

Expensive

- **Andre's**, 401 S. Sixth St. (702/385-5016)
- **Skye Room**, **Binion's Horseshoe Hotel** (702/382-1600). The food is good, but the great views of the city is the main reason to come here.
- **Aristocrat**, 850 S. Rancho (702/870-1977)
- **Elaine's**, **Golden Nugget** (702/385-7111)

Moderate

- **Swiss Cafe**, 1431 E. Charleston - not far from Downtown (702/382-6444). Nice views of the city.
- **Burgundy Room**, **Lady Luck Hotel** (702/477-3000)

GREATER LAS VEGAS

Moderate

- **Cafe Nicolle**, 4760 W. Sahara Ave. (702/870-7675)
- **Philip's Supper House**, 4545 W. Sahara (702/873-5222)

ITALIAN/PIZZA

THE STRIP

Expensive

- **Romeo's**, 2800 W. Sahara (702/873-5400)
- **Primavera**, **Caesars Palace** (702/731-7568)

Moderate

- **Alta Villa**, **Flamingo Hilton** (702/733-3111)
- **Antonio's**, **Rio Hotel** (702/252-7777)
- **DiMartino's**, 2797 S. Maryland Pkwy (702/732-1817). Off the Strip.
- **Fratelli Ristorante**, 3311 E. Flamingo (702/458-5555). Off the Strip.

Inexpensive
- **Olive Garden**, 1545 E. Flamingo (702/735-0082). Pizza.
- **Battista's Hole in the Wall**, 4041 Audrie (702/733-3950). Pizza. Across from Bally's Hotel.

DOWNTOWN

Expensive
- **Stefano's**, **Golden Nugget** (702/385-7111)

Moderate
- **Chicago Joe's**, **Fitzgerald's Hotel** (702/382-5246)
- **California Pizza Kitchen**, **Golden Nugget** (702/385-7111)
- **Pasta Pirate**, **California Hotel** (702/285-1222). Good seafood too.

GREATER LAS VEGAS

Expensive
- **Cipriani**, 2790 E. Flamingo (702/369-6711)

Moderate
- **Bootlegger**, 5025 S. Eastern Ave at Tropicana (702/736-4939). Pizza's your best bet here.
- **Carluccio's Tivoli Gardens**, 1775 E. Tropicana (702/795-3236)
- **The Venetian**, 3713 W. Sahara (702/876-4190)

Inexpensive
- **Sicilian Cafe**, 3510 E. Tropicana (702/456-1300)
- **Pasta Mia**, 2585 E. Flamingo (702/733-0091)

ASSORTED ETHNIC

THE STRIP

Expensive
- **Hakase**, 3900 Paradise Rd. (702/796-1234). Japanese. Good fresh sushi.
- **Chin's**, 3200 Las Vegas Blvd. S. (in the Fashion Show Mall). Szechuan Chinese.
- **Ginza**, 1000 E. Sahara (702/732-3080). Japanese.
- **Ah'So**, **Caesars Palace** (702/731-7731). Japanese.
- **Empress Court, Caesars Palace** (702/731-7110). Chinese.

Moderate
- **Yolie's**, 3900 Paradise Rd. (702/794-0700). Brazilian steak house.
- **Alpine Village**, 3003 Paradise Rd. (702/734-6888). German.
- **South Korean BBQ**, 953 E. Sahara (702/369-4123). Korean.
- **Lotus of Siam**, 953 E. Sahara Ave. (702/735-4477). Thai.
- **Shalimar**, 3900 Paradise Rd., (702-796-0302). Indian; another location several miles west of the Strip at 2605 S. Decatur Blvd. (702/252-8320).
- **Tokyo**, 953 E. Sahara (702/735-7070). Japanese.
- **A Touch of Ginger**, 4110 S. Maryland Pkwy (702/796-1779). Vietnamese.

Inexpensive
- **Margarita's Cantina**, **Frontier Hotel** (702/794-8200). Mexican.
- **Komol**, 953 E. Sahara (702/731-6542). Thai.

- **Tony's Greco-Roman**, 220 W. Sahara (702/384-5171). Greek (and some Italian).
- **Bagelmania**, 855 E. Twain, not far from the Strip (702/369-3322).

NOTE: Komol, South Korean BBQ, Lotus of Siam, and Tokyo are all located in the Commercial Center complex, about a mile from the Strip along Sahara Ave. Ginza is across the street from the Commercial Center.

DOWNTOWN

Expensive
- **Lillie Langtrey's**, **Golden Nugget** (702/385-7111). Cantonese Chinese.

Moderate
- **Emperor's Room**, **Lady Luck Hotel** (702/477-3000). Chinese.

Inexpensive
- **El Sombrero**, 807 S. Main St. (702/382-9234). Mexican.

GREATER LAS VEGAS

Moderate
- **Cathay House**, 5300 Spring Mt. Rd. (702/876-3838). Dim Sum is the specialty here.
- **Baja**, 8331 E. Tropicana (702/458-7300). Southwestern fare.
- **Ricardo's**, *three locations:* 4930 W. Flamingo (702/871-7119); 2389 E. Tropicana (702/798-4515); Meadows Mall (702/870-1088). Mexican.
- **Saigon**, 4251 W. Sahara Ave. (702/362-9978). Vietnamese.

- **Bamboo Garden**, 4850 W. Flamingo (702/871-3262). Chinese (different styles).
- **Fuji**, 3430 E. Tropicana (702/435-8838). Japanese.
- **Waldemar's**, 2202 W. Charleston (702/386-1995). German.
- **India King**, 2202 W. Charleston. In the Rancho Shopping Plaza (702/385-7977). Indian.
- **Jerusalem Restaurant and Deli**, 1305 Vegas Valley Dr. (702/735-2878). Kosher Jewish Deli and Israeli cuisine.

Inexpensive
- **Willy & Jose's**, **Sam's Town Hotel** (702/454-8044). Mexican.
- **Golden Wok**, 4760 S. Eastern (702/456-1868) or 504 S. Decatur (702/878-1596). Both Szechuan and Cantonese Chinese.
- **Macayo Vegas**, 1741 E. Charleston (702/382-5605). Mexican.
- **Vega's Cafe**, 4367 W. Charleston (702/870-7411). Mexican.
- **Fong's**, 2021 E. Charleston (702/382-1644). One of the original Cantonese restaurants in Vegas.

11. EXCURSIONS AND DAY TRIPS

If you've come all this way to Las Vegas and never leave the Strip, you'll be missing one of the most beautiful parts of the country. You don't have to travel all the way to the Grand Canyon to see some breathtaking sights - they're all around you, most within an hours' drive or less. The purple hues of Mt. Charleston in twilight, the incredible workmanship of Hoover Dam, the stillness of an early morning mist in Valley of Fire State Park - these scenes are not what leap to mind when your friend or loved one says to you: "Let's go to Vegas."

But the majesty of the Southwest's mountains and canyons is also Vegas, perhaps not as much as the neon and glitz of Casinoland, but almost. The area attractions are as exciting and interesting as you'll find anywhere. Our strong recommendation is to take a spin out to some of the sights and soak up a day or two of the great outdoors.

Depending on your travel style, you can either rent a car and see the sights yourself, or go on one of the many tours that depart Las Vegas for area excursions. A number of the tours can be done in well under a day, while some are two days or more. We'll show you all the possibilities in this chapter.

LAS VEGAS AREA EXCURSIONS MAP

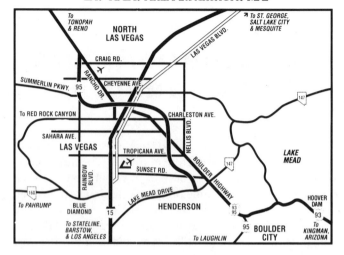

TOURS AND TOURIST INFORMATION

If you decide you want someone else to do the work, contact one of the many tour operators around town. Many hotels have information about tours or have excursion desks in the lobby, and they too will be more than happy to set something up for you. If you want some basic tour information before you arrive, call or write the **Las Vegas Convention and Visitors Authority**, 3150 Paradise Rd., Las Vegas, NV 89109 (702/892-0711).

Check your hotel lobby for bus or plane tour information to most area excursions.

TRAVEL DISTANCES TO AREA EXCURSIONS

Hoover Dam	30 miles
Lake Mead Marina	38 miles
Grand Canyon North Rim	307 miles
Grand Canyon South Rim	290 miles
Valley of Fire State Park	52 miles
Red Rock Canyon	16 miles
Spring Mountain State Park	20 miles
Bonnie Springs Ranch	19 miles
Mt. Charleston	34 miles
Laughlin	90 miles

HOOVER DAM

Hoover Dam, about 45 minutes away by car, is one of the great architectural triumphs of the early twentieth century, and remains Nevada's top tourist draw. The dam, known for its first twelve years as Boulder Dam, provides between four and five *billion* kilowatt-hours of electricity a year to three states: Nevada, Arizona, and California.

Located in Boulder City - the one city in Nevada where gambling is illegal - a visit to Hoover Dam is a must-see for visitors who want to see more than three kings and a pair of tens (well, that would be pretty nice too).

The dam is 726 feet high with a base 660 feet thick. It's made of seven million tons of concrete and 18 million tons of reinforced steel. Thousands of workers labored five years and 94 construction workers died before the Dam was finished in 1935. In 1955, the American Society of Civil Engineers officially declared it one of the seven engineering wonders of the world.

The mighty **Colorado River**, responsible for the shape of the Grand Canyon, is diverted here and the dammed-up result is **Lake Mead** (see below).

You can take tours inside (highly recommended) or outside the Dam, view a movie about the history of the project, and see other exhibits in the **Exhibit Center** (702/ 293-8367). An elevator takes you to the lower depths, and you can see the 17 huge turbines and other generating equipment up close.

The **Boulder City/Hoover Dam Museum**, in Boulder City, has a good collection of historical exhibits from the Dam's early history, and also shows a movie about the Dam's construction. Contact the **Hoover Dam Visitors Bureau** for more information at 1228 Arizona St., Boulder City, NV 89005 (702/294-1988).

En route to the Dam from Vegas, do yourself a favor and stop for breakfast, lunch, or coffee at the **Coffee Cup**, a great little joint that seems like it hasn't changed since the late 1940's, located at 558 Nevada Highway in Boulder City (702/294-0517). The pancakes and french toast are delicious, the service friendly and efficient.

DIRECTIONS: Take the Boulder Highway (the name changes to Nevada Highway as you approach the Dam) all the way from Vegas, about 30 miles.

LAKE MEAD

The Lake Mead National Recreation Area (601 Nevada Highway, Boulder City, NV 89005; 702/293-8920) is the byproduct of the Hoover Dam project, and a darn nice byproduct at that. In addition to providing aquatic relief from hot summers, Lake Mead, the largest man-made lake in the Western Hemisphere, supplies water to 25 million people throughout Nevada and the Southwest. Las Vegas gets most of its water from Lake Mead by way of the **Southern Nevada Water Project**.

Lake Mead begins about 25 miles from Las Vegas and snakes as far away as 100 miles to **Cottonnwood Cove**. The lake has 550 miles of shoreline for you to enjoy fishing, boating (there are six marinas), rafting, other water sports and camping. It reaches into the Lower Grand Canyon when full. If you're going to fish, you'll need a license. Fishermen will be pleased to learn the variety of fish in Lake Mead: largemouth bass, striped bass, catfish, crappie, trout, and bluegill.

If cruising along the lake in a paddle boat strikes your fancy, contact **Lake Mead Cruises**, 1646 Nevada Highway, Boulder City; 702/293-6180). The boats leave from Lake Mead Marina (322 Lakeshore Rd., Boulder City; 702/293-3484). Dinner/dance cruises are available aboard the *Desert Princess*. You can also rent boats here or eat at the famous floating restaurant. Go to **Boulder Beach** for good diving and swimming.

You can also go rafting on Lake Mead with the **Black Canyon River Raft Tour** (702/293-3776 or 800/845-3833).

See page 193 in the *Fun in the Sun* chapter for more information.

DIRECTIONS: Same as to Hoover Dam: take the Boulder Highway (the name changes to Nevada Highway) all the way from Vegas, about 38 miles to the Lake Mead Marina.

GRAND CANYON

You're close to the most majestic piece of real estate in the US of A, but it's not around the corner. The North Rim is roughly 307 miles from Vegas, the South Rim 290 miles. To call the Grand Canyon a "Las Vegas area attraction" is analogous to New York calling Washington, DC, or Boston "New York area attractions." Still, who can blame the city pols for wanting to claim the Grand Canyon as their very own backyard?

The Canyon runs 277 miles in length, is a mile deep, and almost 20 miles across at its widest point. It's a breathtaking, beautiful place, wilderness preservation at its very best. We're assuming here that you're mainly interested in a brief visit, so we'll limit our remarks here to the very basics since huge volumes exist on the history, attractions, lodging, etc. For those of you planning longer stays, call the **Grand Canyon Lodge** for North Rim information (602/638-7864) or the **Grand Canyon Visitor Center** for information about the whole national park area (602/638-7888).

Helicopter and Plane Tours

If you're like growing numbers of Vegas tourists, you'll seriously consider one of the "flight-seeing" plane or helicopter tour services. Departing out of either McCarran International Airport or Sky Harbor Airport (Highway 146, six miles south of the city), they fly over Hoover Dam, Lake Mead, and one or both rims of the Grand Canyon. Some airlines and helicopters also offer overflights of Bryce Canyon in Utah, Zion National Park, and Indian Country (Grand Canyon West Rim). Depending on how long you're airborne, the cost will run you anywhere from $79 a person to $200-$300 for overnight trips. Group discounts are usually available.

The main flight-seeing air services are:

- **Air Nevada** (702/736-8900; 800/634-6377)
- **Adventure Airlines** (702/736-7511; 800/543-3077)
- **Lake Mead Air** (702/293-1848)
- **Las Vegas Airlines** (702/735-8007; 800/634-6851)
- **Scenic Airlines** (702/739-1900; 800/634-6801)
- **Sierra Nevada Air** (702/736-6770)
- **Western Airlines** (702/891-0041)

For helicopters, try:

- **Helicop-Tours** (702/736-0606), or
- **Grand Canyon West** (702/736-7511; 800/543-3077), who also offer plane and bus tours.

If you prefer to drive or take a bus to the Grand Canyon, you can also sign up for airplane and helicopter tours once you get there.

Bus Tours

Speaking of bus tours, most depart in the morning and return by dinner time. **Guaranteed Tours** (702/369-1000; 800/777-6555) goes to the Grand Canyon, Lake Mead, Hoover Dam and includes an Indian barbecue for $99.50. **Interstate Tours** (702/293-2268; 800/245-1166) will take you to Grand Canyon West, where you can traipse around the **Hualapai Indian Reservation**, and view the Joshua

Tree forest in the Grand Canyon's Indian Country. Call **Gray Line** (702/384-1234) for their combined land and air tour.

DIRECTIONS: To the North Rim, take Rt. 15 east to Rt. 9 east, then south on Rt. 89 at Mount Carmel; take the Rt. 67 turn-off and follow it to the end. **To the South Rim**, take Rt. 93 south to Rt. 40 east; take Rt. 64/Rt. 180 north.

VALLEY OF FIRE STATE PARK

If you're going to hike or camp, hunt for old rocks, or just contemplate the nature of the Earth's geological history, this is the place to do it. Red sandstone juts out in all directions, creating a picture-perfect desert landscape of rock formations with names like **Mouse's Tank**, **Seven Sisters**, and **Elephant Rock**. Look for the bighorn sheep, burros, and other Southwestern animals roaming about.

If you're hiking, you'll want to rest and take in the view at **The Cabins**, built by the CCC (Civilian Conservation Corps) in 1935 out of local sandstone. Fifty thousand year-old petroglyphs and beautiful examples of petrified wood abound here. Visit the **Silica Dome** for a very unusual white sand structure and the **Atlatl Rock** for prehistoric rock art.

Stop by the **Visitor Center** (702/397-2088) for trail maps, exhibits, and books on the park. The view from the Visitor Center, by the way, is well worth the trip out, so even if you don't intend to walk around, go see the Center. You can also drive through the park if you're in a lazy mood. Valley of Fire is about 52 miles northeast of Vegas outside of Overton. The **Lost City Museum** in Overton is a small but fine museum specializing in Anasazi Indian artifacts from the days of the Muddy River habitation - a long, long time ago.

DIRECTIONS: Take I-15 north about one hour (roughly 45 miles). The state park exit will take you right in.

RED ROCK CANYON

Less than a half-hour drive west of town you'll find some of the most beautiful red sandstone and gray limestone formations and cliff outcroppings ever carved by water and wind erosion. Part of the Spring Mountains, Red Rock Canyon was formerly home to the Paiute Indians. The sunlight at different times of the day changes the hues, so that the Canyon area is always a little different each time you come here.

To begin with, stop in at the **Red Rock Visitors Center** (1000 Scenic Dr.; 702/363-1921) to get trail guides and maps, view exhibits, look at books on local plants and wildlife, and get general park information (Red Rock Canyon is a national conservation area administered by the Bureau of Land Management, a part of the Department of the Interior). The sandstone and limestone come together at the **Keystone Thrust**, a fault or fracture where the ancient rocks collided with (and are now superimposed on top of) one another. The escarpment runs for 15 miles, is about 3,000 feet high, and was probably created about the time the dinosaurs died out - 65 million years ago.

Red Rock Canyon has nature trails, more strenuous hiking trails, a one-way loop drive for cars 13 miles long, and lots of great spots for rock climbing. Off the beaten track a bit you should be able to see bighorn sheep, burros, horses, antelope and the endangered desert tortoise. Two of our favorite hikes are through the **Calico Hills** and the **Sandstone Quarry**. If you're visiting with children, take them along the short **Children's Discovery Trail**, where they'll learn about different varieties of plants and trees, and see where Indians used to live beneath the natural rock overhangs. The park measures 10 miles by 16 miles.

DIRECTIONS: Head west on West Charleston Blvd. (Downtown) for about 16 miles and follow sign to Red Rock Canyon.

SPRING MOUNTAIN RANCH STATE PARK

The park lies within Red Rock Canyon recreation lands, and the main attraction here, apart from the great views, is the **Ranch House** lying below the reddish **Wilson Cliff Range** and the wildlife-rich **Lake Harriet**. The 500-plus acre ranch, built in 1869 and added to through the years, has been owned by Howard Hughes and other notables. The state sponsors special events and activities, particularly the much-loved **Theater Under the Stars** summer concerts on the lawn in front of the house.

DIRECTIONS: Same as to Red Rock Canyon, but continue on Rt. 159 (W. Charleston Blvd.) for several miles. You'll see the sign for Spring Mountain Ranch.

BONNIE SPRINGS RANCH

Just a few miles past Red Rock Canyon is Bonnie Springs Ranch (1 Gunfighter Ln., 702/875-4191). Built in 1843, the ranch was used as a wagon-train stop along the Old Spanish Trail to California. A good place to bring kids, the ranch has a petting and feeding zoo and offers horseback riding. Adjacent to the ranch is **Old Nevada Village**, a restoration of an Old West frontier town with wooden sidewalks and saloons, ice cream parlors, a blacksmith shop, museums and shops. Kids will love the miniature train ride, the gunfights, and the hangings out on the main street.

DIRECTIONS: Same as to Red Rock Canyon, but continue on Rt. 159 (W. Charleston Blvd.) for three miles.

MOUNT CHARLESTON
AND TOIYABE NATIONAL FOREST

A scant half-hour trip north of town will put you in the **Toiyabe National Forest**, where most of the year you'll find great hiking, camping, backpacking, wagon rides, horseback riding, and in the winter you can go skiing and sleigh-riding. There is abundant wildlife (including coyotes, bighorn sheep, cougar, and deer) and several dozen species of plant life here, so much so that you'll wonder whether you're really still just a hop, skip, and a jump away from all that blazing neon.

The mountains reach over 10,000 feet in the Spring Mountain Range, which of course affects the weather: be forewarned that it often gets chilly at night. Imposing **Mt. Charleston** rises to 11,918 feet, and should take you about an hour to reach from Las Vegas. Whether you're gazing at the area's tallest peak, or looking out below and beyond from up top, the view is spectacular.

Campers can drive to a campsite and do their thing from May 1 through September 30 only, although you can winter camp if you walk in. There are some beautiful trails here, several of which originate behind the **Mt. Charleston Lodge**, which is not an accommodations place but rather an eating place, and a popular one at that. In the winter, the Lodge offers sleigh rides. If you want to stay in the area for the night, and you're not a camper, the only place to go is the **Mt. Charleston Hotel**, which is a very nice place.

For complete information on all the trails, including advice on trail difficulty levels and weather conditions, as well as activities in the Forest, call the **Ranger Station** (702/872-5486). If you plan to tackle Mt. Charleston, the rangers can help you out. Off Rt. 158 (Deer Creek Highway), spend a few minutes at the **Desert View Scenic Outlook** for an impressive view of the Las Vegas Valley. The Forest has the best local cross-country skiing, and **Lee Canyon Ski Area** on Rt. 156 (702/872-5462 or 646-0008), 47 miles from town, has the best downhill skiing in southern Nevada.

DIRECTIONS: Drive about a half-hour north on US-95 until you hit the Kyle Canyon Turnoff and take Kyle Canyon Road (Rt. 157). Another 15 minutes up Kyle Canyon Road you'll hit the Mt. Charleston Hotel and just beyond that you'll find the town, about 34 miles from Vegas. For skiers without cars, call the **Lee Canyon Bus** at 702/646-0008.

LAUGHLIN

Many Vegas tour operators offer you a chance to do the exact same thing you'd do in Vegas - gamble - in the small town of Laughlin, some 90 miles to the south. But Laughlin is not just a smaller version of Vegas. It's got the Colorado River flowing through town, separating Nevada's southern-most city from Bullhead City, Arizona on the eastern bank of the river, and that means a wide variety of water fun right in front of you.

Most Vegas hotels have literature on Laughlin excursions in their lobby; you might want to check out **Gray Line's** daytrips (702/384-1234; 800/634-6579); **Ray & Ross** (702/646-4661; 800/338-8111); or **Guaranteed Tours** (702/369-1000).

Las Vegas is not the only southern Nevada town with a nearby dam: Laughlin has **Davis Dam** at the edge of town, holding back the Colorado River to the south and Lake Mohave to the north. From desert oasis just a decade back - there were only 90 residents in 1983 - to today's construction boom, Laughlin has come a long way. There are now more than 10,000 hotel rooms, and ten major hotel/

casinos, almost all of which are Las Vegas offshoots: Harrah's, Golden Nugget, Pioneer, Flamingo Hilton, and so on.

One of the more fun hotel/casinos to visit is **The Colorado Belle**, a recreation of an old Mississippi paddlewheeler anchored on the banks of Laughlin's Colorado River (2100 Casino Dr., Laughlin, NV 89029, 702/298-4000; 800/458-9500). A Dixieland band provides entertainment in the **River Boat Lounge** at night. The Colorado Belle is owned by Circus Circus. At the **Riverside Resort** (1650 S. Casino Dr.; 702/298-2535), go C&W dancing at the **Western Dance Hall**. Riverside golfing is available at **Harrah's** and the new **Emerald River Golf Course** (1155 S. Casino Dr.; 702/298-0061), rated Nevada's most challenging golf course by the United States Golf Association (USGA).

Hotel construction continues apace, fed by ever increasing numbers of tourists who now make Laughlin either their only destination or at least a side trip for a day or two. Gambling is the main activity, of course, but tourists and many southern Nevadans like the idea of outdoor fun being within easy reach (not that Las Vegas outdoor excursions are difficult to get to; it's just much closer in here). Fishing, swimming, boating, and various water sports are all just a few minutes away on the Colorado. For more information on hotels, casinos, and events, contact the **Laughlin Visitor Center** (1555 Casino Dr.; 702/298-3321).

DIRECTIONS: Take US-93/95 south about 90 minutes to Rt. 163 (east), then into Laughlin.

GHOST TOWNS

Most of southern Nevada's ghost towns were once thriving silver, lead, or zinc mining centers, sprung up to support the mining industry. The prosperity, however, was short-lived. Many of these towns did not last very long at all, places like **Potosi**, **Sandy**, and **Searchlight**. The main ghost town close by we'd recommend (most of the other ghost towns have little or nothing to show for themselves) is **Goodsprings**, 35 miles southwest of Las Vegas.

The combination of a natural spring and the wanderings of one Joseph Good combined to fix the town's name. Good mined the area for a while in 1861, but soon left. In 1886, prospectors from Utah set up camp, and soon there were more than 40 mines established. By the early 1900's, Goodsprings was a hopping place, something of a regional hub, with several thousand residents living in or near town. But in 1918, a flu epidemic took many lives, followed soon after by the collapse of metal and mineral prices. About 100 people still call Goodsprings their home. The big tourist attraction is the old **Pioneer Saloon**.

DIRECTIONS: Take I-15 south to Jean, turn west on Rt. 161 for seven miles to Goodsprings.

INDIAN RESERVATIONS

Visitors to Las Vegas who are interested in things Indian will be disappointed. While there are some great museums (particularly the Lost City Museum in Overton and the Natural History Museum in Las Vegas), there is not the same kind of tourist infrastructure on southern Nevada reservations that there is in neighboring states. Depending on your attitude towards these things, this is either good (Native Americans are not reduced to tourist attractions) or bad (opportunity for interaction and understanding between the two cultures is reduced).

Three Indian nations have lived in Nevada for hundreds of years at least, if not thousands: the Shoshone; Washoe; and Paiute. There are more than 25 reservations in the state, totaling 1.3 million acres of land. Two are in Clark County: one in Las Vegas, just off the Strip, which is not much more than a small trailer park; and the **Moapa Reservation**, about an hour north of town. Again, other than the fireworks stand by the side of the road, there's not much to do or see here of an activities nature. The Moapa and other tribes occasionally hold pow-wows and perform ceremonial dances in Las Vegas and Boulder City.

DIRECTIONS: To get to Moapa Reservation, take I-15 north about 45 miles or so; take the Valley of Fire State Park exit.

CAMPING

A number of good campgrounds are located throughout the area. In the Toiyabe National Forest, check out the **Kyle Canyon Campgrounds** (off of Rt. 157) and the **Dolomite Campgrounds** (off of Rt. 156 in the Lee Canyon area). Hard by Dolomite you'll find the **Hilltop Campground** and **McWilliams Campground** (both located off Rt. 156). Call the US Forest Service for details and fees at 702/873-8800 (at last check, the overnight fees were $7). You have several campgrounds to choose from in the Lake Mead area. Two of the better camp sites (better being a very relative term here) are **Boulder Beach** (702/293-8906) and the **Las Vegas Boat Harbor** (702/565-9111).

Near Laughlin, on the Arizona side, you can camp at **Katherine Landing** (602/754-3272), a public beach a few miles up from Davis Dam on the shores of Lake Mohave. On the Nevada side, camp facilities can be found at **Sportsman's Park** (Rt. 163 and Casino Dr.).

188

12. FUN IN THE SUN

Few other major cities in the US offer the variety of major sports and recreation activities, including professional and collegiate sporting events, as does Las Vegas. And when you throw into the mix the world's best gambling, great getaways and excursions, and all the fabulous, wacky mega-resorts, you've got a town that's a heck of a good time for both young and old.

Whichever sport you like to play, or whatever sport you like to watch, you should have no trouble finding something fun to suit your needs.

GOLF

The Vegas area has some of the finest golfing in the Southwest. There are 23 major golf clubs, private and public, including Boulder City and one of the very best (Peppermill Palms) in Mesquite, about 77 miles northeast near the Utah border. The LPGA plays here, and for the last ten years so has the Las Vegas Invitational Golf Tournament.

These are the main golf courses in Vegas and nearby. Call first to find out about greens fees, course difficulty, and other necessities.

- **Angel Park Golf Club**, 100 S. Rampart Blvd. (702/254-4653)
- **Black Mountain Golf & Country Club**, 501 Country Club Dr., Henderson (702/565-7933).

- **Boulder City Municipal Golf Course**, 1 Clubhouse Dr., Boulder City (702/293-9236)
- **Calvada Golf and Country Club**, 8706 Canyon View Dr. (702/363-0481). Private.
- **Craig Ranch Golf Course**, 628 W. Craig Rd. (702/642-9700)
- **Desert Inn Country Club**, 3145 Las Vegas Blvd. S. (702/733-4299)
- **Desert Rose Golf Course**, 5843 Club House Dr. (438-4653)
- **Las Vegas Country Club**, 3000 Joe W. Brown Dr. (702/734-1122). Private.
- **Las Vegas Golf Club**, 4349 Vegas Dr. (702/646-3003)
- **Legacy Golf Club**, 130 Par Excellence Dr. (702/897-2187)
- **Los Prados Golf and Country Club**, 5150 Los Prados Circle (702/645-5696)
- **Mirage Golf Club**, at the former Dunes Golf and Country Club, 3650 Las Vegas Blvd. S. (702/369-7111)
- **North Las Vegas Community Course**, 324 E. Brooks Ave., N. Las Vegas (702/649-7171)
- **Painted Desert Country Club**, 5555 Painted Mirage Way (702/645-2568)
- **Peppermill Palms Golf Course**, 1134 Mesquite Blvd., Mesquite, NV (800/621-0187)
- **Royal Kenfield Country Club**, 1 Showboat Country Club Dr. (702/434-9000)
- **Sahara Country Club**, 1911 E. Desert Inn Rd. (702/796-0013)
- **Spanish Trail Golf and Country Club**, 5050 Spanish Trail Ln. (702/364-5050). Private.
- **Sun City Summerlin Golf Club**, 9201-B Del Webb Blvd. (702/363-4373). Semi-private.

- **Sunrise Country Club**, 5500 E. Flamingo (702/456-3160). Private.
- **Sunrise Vista Golf Course at Nellis**, Nellis Air Force Base, Building T-1619 (702/459-7908)
- **Tournament Players Club at Summerlin**, 1700 Village Center Dr. (702/791-4382)

MINIATURE GOLF

And don't forget the **miniature golf courses**. Two of the better mini-golf experiences are at **Premier Golf Services**, 5030 Paradise Rd. (702/597-2794) and **Scandia Family Fun Center**, 2900 Sirius Rd. (702/364-0070).

TENNIS

There are more than 200 tennis courts in and around the city. Many of the hotels offer tennis courts, particularly on the Strip, but priority is usually given to guests.

Hotel Tennis Courts

Listed alphabetically, the hotels that offer tennis are:
- **Aladdin**, 3667 Las Vegas Blvd. S. (702/736-0111). Two lighted outdoor courts.
- **Alexis Park**, 375 E. Harmon Ave. (702/796-3300). Two lighted outdoor courts.
- **Bally's**, 3645 Las Vegas Blvd. S. (702/739-4111). Ten outdoor courts, five lighted.
- **Caesars Palace**, 3570 Las Vegas Blvd. S. (702/731-7786). Four outdoor courts.
- **Desert Inn**, 3145 Las Vegas Blvd. S. (702/733-4444). Ten outdoor courts, five lighted.
- **Flamingo Hilton**, 3555 Las Vegas Blvd. S. (702/733-3111). Four outdoor lighted courts.
- **Frontier**, 3120 Las Vegas Blvd. S. (702/794-8200). Two

lighted outdoor courts.
- **Hacienda**, 3950 Las Vegas Blvd. S. (702/739-8911). Six courts, two lighted.
- **Las Vegas Hilton**, 3000 Paradise Rd. (702/732-5111). Six lighted outdoor courts. Guests only.
- **Jackie Gaughan's Plaza Hotel**, 1 Main St. (702/386-2110). Four lighted outdoor courts.
- **Riviera**, 2901 Las Vegas Blvd. S. (702/734-5110). Two lighted outdoor courts.
- **Tropicana**, 3801 Las Vegas Blvd. S. (702/739-2222). Four lighted outdoor courts.

Public and Private Tennis Courts

Outside of hotels, public courts are to be found all over, at parks, schools, and tennis centers. Some of the better courts around town are:
- **Angel Park**, Westcliff and Durango (702/255-9515).
- **Jaycee Park**, St. Louis and Eastern Avenues (702/386-6297).
- **Las Vegas Racquet Club**, 3333 W. Raven (702/361-2202). Six outdoor lighted courts. Private.
- **Sports Club**, 3025 Industrial Rd. (702/733-8999). Two outdoor lighted courts (nine indoor racquetball courts).
- **Studio 96**, 3896 Swenson Ave. (702/735-8153). Ten indoor courts; four outdoor lighted courts.
- **Twin Lakes Racquet Club**, 3075 W. Washington Blvd. (702/647-3434). Eight outdoor lighted courts.
- **UNLV**, 4505 S. Maryland Pkwy (702/739-3150). Twelve outdoor lighted courts.

SKIING AND ICE SKATING

Even though few people think of winter sports when

planning a trip to Vegas, if you're here in the colder
months, two possibilities are skiing and skating. There are
only two places to go, but they are more than adequate to
the task. For cross-country and alpine skiing, head north to
the Mount Charleston area in the Toiyabe National Forest
to the **Lee Canyon Ski Area** on Rt. 156 (702/872-5462 or
646-0008), 47 miles from town. Three double chair lifts
service Lee Canyon's three slopes, where you'll encounter
runs named Highroller, Blackjack, Keno, and Slot Alley!
Base elevation is 8,500 feet.

For ice skating, go to the **Santa Fe Hotel** (4949 N.
Rancho; 702/658-4991) and skate to your hearts' content at
the NHL regulation rink.

BOWLING

Las Vegas has nine major bowling centers, several of
which are in the following hotels:

- **Arizona Charlie's**, 740 S. Decatur Blvd. (702/258-5200).
- **Gold Coast**, 4000 W. Flamingo (702/367-7111).
- **Sam's Town Bowling Center**, 5111 Boulder Highway
  (702/456-7777).
- **Santa Fe Hotel**, 4949 N. Rancho (702/658-4900). Only
  bowling lanes in town with "Bowlervision."
- **Showboat Bowling Lanes**, 2800 E. Fremont (702/385-
  9123).

Not attached to a hotel, **West Hill Lanes** at 4747 W.
Charleston Blvd. (702/878-9711) is another good bowling
spot, a bit removed from Glitter Gulch.

BUNGEE JUMPING

Okay, so there aren't a lot of places that offer bungee
jumping yet, but it's just a matter of time before more
bungee opportunities arise. For now, satisfy your jumping

needs at **Bungee Masters**, 810 Circus Circus Dr. (702/385-4321), adjacent to Circus Circus. Bungee Masters' motto is *Carpe Diem*, Latin for *Seize the Day*. The Sky Tower is 201 feet high, they have a double bungee deck and, of course, a bungee elevator to lift you to the jump site. Group rates and night jumps available. The price is $59 for one jump, $89 for a double jump. Look out below!

RAFTING

In Lake Mohave due south of Hoover Dam, you can take the **Black Canyon River Raft Tour**, 3 1/2 hours of floating fun. The trip begins at the base of Hoover Dam and winds past some of the most stunning canyon lands you'll ever see. It's a great way to see the magnificent landscape of the Southwest.

If they're not too shy, you'll see bighorn sheep and other desert fauna. Watch for the natural hot springs and swirling whirlpools.   Call 702/293-3776 or 800/845-3833 for times and prices.

BOATING

Boating choices in the greater Las Vegas area are pretty simple: either drive north to Lake Mead, or go south to Laughlin. In the Lake Mead Recreation Area, there are six marinas to choose from. The marina at **Lake Mead Lodge** (322 Lakeshore Rd., Boulder City; 702/293-2074) is very accessible and has a good selection of water-craft.

If you head south to Laughlin, boating is available either on Lake Mohave or on the Colorado River that cuts through town. Call or visit the **Laughlin Visitor Center** (1555 Casino Dr., 702/298-3321).

HORSEBACK RIDING

There's a growing number of stables around, but two of the best require a bit of a ride. We like them in part because the riding trails are very pretty and scenic. Try **Bonnie Springs Ranch** (702/865-4191) for Red Rock Canyon horsing around. The **Mount Charleston Riding Stables** (702/872-7009) offer great vistas of the Mt. Charleston/Toiyabe National Forest area.

MINOR LEAGUE BASEBALL

Las Vegas is home to the San Diego Padres Triple-A minor league franchise, the *Las Vegas Stars*. The *Stars'* season runs a little shorter than the major leaguers, from April to September. Catch them at Cashman Field, 850 Las Vegas Blvd. N.; call 702/386-7200 for the schedule of home games.

UNLV SPORTS

The **Thomas and Mack Center** (seating capacity: 18,000) has become well known to sports fans for boxing matches and the winning University of Nevada at Las Vegas basketball team. Under Jerry Tarkanian, the winningest coach in NCAA history, UNLV racked up one of the most impressive college basketball records ever, including winning the 1990 championship. The Tark is gone, but UNLV's *Runnin' Rebels* remain a force to be reckoned with on the court, in part because Rollie Massimino of Villanova fame is the new head coach. For tickets, call 702/739-3267).

UNLV's other *Rebels* are of the football variety. They play at the **Sam Boyd Silver Bowl** (7000 E. Russell Rd.; 702/739-3900). Their record has not been as stellar as the school's basketball team, but they periodically rise to the occasion and kick some booty.

UNIVERSITY OF NEVADA AT LAS VEGAS

Known to many people for its winning basketball teams and its flamboyant towel-chewing former coach, Jerry Tarkanian, UNLV actually has a good academic program too. The campus, spread out over 335 acres, has more than 18,000 students enrolled. The Thomas and Mack Arena on campus hosts many athletic events, conventions, and other large activities. The university is one of the few to offer a School of Hotel Administration, many of whose graduates help run the hotels and casinos in Las Vegas, Reno, and Laughlin.

---

13. KIDSTUFF

Las Vegas is no longer the last place you'd ever want to drag your kids. On the contrary, the phrase "good clean fun" can now be used in reference to Vegas without eliciting huge peals of laughter from tour operators, veteran gamblers, or Joe Cowboy in town for a little rodeo action. Since the late 1970's, Vegas has been invaded by big corporate types who see the Disney World profit margins and muse about the next kiddie-theme mega-resort - and thank God for it!

Whether your family is into water fun, circus acts, carnivals, white tigers, or magic shows, there's plenty to do for those of you with kids or those of you who remain young at heart. We'll start with a few hotels that cater to families big-time.

FAMILY-FRIENDLY HOTELS

Far and away, Circus Circus Enterprises - owners of Circus Circus, Excalibur, Luxor, and Grand Slam Canyon - has the kiddie's market sown up, though there's heavy competition coming their way from the MGM Grand and Treasure Island. While the new hotels will almost certainly cut into Circus Circus's hide, the folks running these places have mastered the art of responding to the needs and whims of America's vacationing kiddie corps.

The most family-friendly hotels are:

· **Circus Circus**, 2880 Las Vegas Blvd. S. (702/734-0410; 800/634-3450). Perhaps the quintessential Vegas hotel oriented to kiddie entertainment, Circus Circus has continual circus acts going on up above the gaming tables, a large video arcade area, and a carnival with all sorts of games. The addition of Grand Slam Canyon, with water rides and roller coasters, adds to the hotel's reputation as an innovator on the Vegas scene.

· **Excalibur,** 3850 Las Vegas Blvd. S. (702/597-7777; 800/937-7777). Another Circus Circus property, Excalibur's motif is medieval days of yore. The dinner show is geared toward the kids, with jousts and horse play of all sorts. There's a small carnival here too, beneath the lobby, and there are those fantastic Magic Motion Machines, where you sit in a small movie theater while the seats move about on hydraulic pumps. It's got to be experienced.

· **Las Vegas Hilton**, 3000 Paradise Rd. (702/732-5111; 800/732-7117). The Youth Hotel offers overnight accommodations or hourly supervision at reasonable rates. Adult-supervised activities and sports are included. Guests at the Flamingo Hilton are also eligible for this service.

· The **MGM Grand and Theme Park** and Mirage's **Treasure Island Hotel** will also be geared towards kids, although MGM in particular will have plenty of grown-up things to do too considering its casino space will be the largest in the world.

A number of other hotels try to find things for kids to do, but few have progressed beyond opening up some video arcade space. **Bally's** has a Youth Center which is very nice, but it's really just a large video arcade with an ice cream parlor attached.

BABYSITTING SERVICES

For those of you lugging along infants and toddlers, you'll need to find a babysitting service. If you're not staying at a hotel that has babysitting, call **Sandy's Sitter Service** (953 E. Sahara; 702/731-2086). The following hotels provide an in-house babysitting service, but call first and find out the details, including price, references, etc.

The first four are on or just off the Strip; the Showboat is near Downtown and Las Vegas Cub is Downtown.

- **The Continental**, 4100 Paradise Rd. (702/737-5555; 800/634-6641).
- **Harrah's Las Vegas**, 3475 Las Vegas Blvd. S. (702/369-5000; 800/634-6765).
- **The Mirage**, 3400 Las Vegas Blvd. S. (702/791-7111; 800/456-7111).
- **Riviera**, 2901 Las Vegas Blvd. S. (702/734-5110; 800/634-6753).
- **Showboat**, 2800 Fremont (702/385-9123; 800/826-2800).
- **Las Vegas Club**, 18 E. Fremont (702/385-1664; 800/634-6532).

MAGIC SHOWS

Las Vegas has a long tradition of magicians plying their craft on-stage. Of course, if you don't follow Avery Cardoza's gambling money-management strategies (see Chapter 6), your money will soon pull a disappearing act on *you*. But seriously, Vegas has some good, some less good, magic acts around, and you and your kids will enjoy the artistry and wonderment of ladies being sawed in half and large animals disappearing before your very eyes.

Even the best shows have some less than satisfying moments, but by and large the following magic shows do a pretty good job. Where a magic show is signed up for an indefinite stay, we note that; otherwise, the hotel is simply listed, meaning that name magicians are booked on a fairly routine basis.

- **Flamingo Hilton**, 3555 Las Vegas Blvd. S. (702/733-3111; 800/732-2111).
- **Hacienda**, 3950 Las Vegas Blvd. S. (702/739-8911; 800/634-6713).
- **Harrah's Las Vegas**, 3475 Las Vegas Blvd. S. (702/369-5000; 800/634-6765), featuring "Lance Burton: A Magical Journey."
- **The Mirage**, 3400 Las Vegas Blvd. S. (702/791-7111; 800/456-7111), featuring Siegfried and Roy and their white tigers and dolphins.
- **Lady Luck**, 206 N. Third St. (702/477-3000; 800/523-9582), featuring "Melinda, First Lady of Magic."
- **San Remo**, 115 E. Tropicana (702/739-9000; 800/522-7366).

SILVER SAFARI YOUTH EXCURSIONS

Silver Safari Youth Excursions is sort of like daycamp for kids on vacation. The excursions are only offered in the summer, between Memorial Day and Labor Day. There are ten safaris, two of which are for children ages six to eight and last five and a half hours. The other safaris are for kids nine to sixteen.

The safaris for older kids last into the evening, and include visits to area museums, horseback riding in the Mt. Charleston range, and some serious splashing at Wet 'n Wild. The price is anywhere from $31.50 to $75.

Silver Safari is certified by the Nevada Public Service Commission. You must sign a medical release and agree to their behavior rules. To sign up, call 702/737-6680 or 800/245-0028 and ask for the Silver Safari information clerk.

SCANDIA FAMILY FUN CENTER

Fun with a Scandinavian twist, you say? Go to the Scandia Family Fun Center at 2900 Sirius Rd. (702/364-0070), located on 1-15 between Sahara and Spring Mountain Roads. Featuring three miniature golf courses, bumper cars, bumper boats, a batting cage, and a video arcad. You can also play some mini-golf and bump the heck out of each other on the "L'il Indy" raceway.

COMPETITION GRAND PRIX GO-CARTS AND FAMILY FUN CENTER

Another family fun center, but this one is really for go-cart enthusiasts only, though there is a game room. The Grand Prix is the largest go-cart track in Nevada, and there's a mini-track for smaller children. If your kids are go-carters, you'll love this place. Located at 2980 S. Sandhill (702/431-7223).

CHILDREN'S MUSEUMS

We're including museums that kids of all ages will enjoy, from six to sixty-six (and older). The **Lied Discovery Children's Museum** (833 Las Vegas Blvd. N., 702/382-5437; admission) is a hands-on, "touch and feel" interactive facility with exhibits teaching children about science, arts, and life.

At the **Four Queens Hotel**, you'll find the **Ripley's Believe It Or Not Museum** (202 E. Fremont St., 702/385-4011; admission). Most of the usual oddball attractions found at other Ripley's Museums are here too - the torture chamber, various and sundry wax figurines, shrunken heads - with some Las Vegas-specific items, like the huge jelly bean roulette wheel.

OTHER MUSEUMS

Both young and old will like the **Las Vegas Natural History Museum** (900 Las Vegas Blvd. N., 702/384-3466; admission). The museum has one animated dinosaur, and they're building another. The fossil record is nicely displayed, with exhibits from the time when dinosaurs ruled the earth to today's animal kingdom. The 300-gallon aquarium is home to several sharks, and there are hundreds of exhibits of birds and animals.

Lied Discovery, Ripley's, and the Natural History Museum are all located Downtown.

The **Marjorie Barrick Museum of Natural History** at the University of Nevada at Las Vegas (UNLV) campus (702/739-3381) is, like the Las Vegas Natural History Museum, more on the highbrow side of things, but this kind of education is also good fun. All manner of living and extinct (and one near-instinct critter, the desert tortoise) flora and fauna can be found here. The most popular attraction here is the huge skeletal remains of the state fossil, the ichthyosaur, a large marine dinosaur.

The **Nevada State Museum and Historical Society** (700 Twin Lakes Dr., 702/486-5205; admission) has exhibits on early Native American social life, desert life, and Nevada's historical developments. There's also a very interesting display on nuclear weapons, given the proximity to the Nevada Test Site (the nation's one and only underground nuclear weapons testing facility). The Nevada State Museum is on the grounds of **Lorenzi Park**, W. Washington Ave. and Twin Lakes Dr., not far from I-95.

THE OLD FORT

The Old Fort (908 Las Vegas Blvd. N., 702/382-7198), the oldest surviving building in Nevada, will give you and your family an idea of how things were when Las Vegas was first occupied by Mormon settlers in 1855. The remaining fort is an adobe structure and has exhibits and artifacts from the early days. An archaeological dig is now in progress.

THE ZOO

On the small side, but still a good zoo, the **Southern Nevada Zoological Park** is a great place to see some wildlife. Located at 1775 N. Rancho Dr. (702/648-5955; admission), the zoo features the usual mix of animals from around the world and around the Southwest. The kids will like the petting zoo. More than 50 species of desert wildlife, particularly reptiles, can be espied here. There is a good collection of different bird species in the Bird Boutique.

ETHEL M

Located in Henderson, is the ever-popular **Ethel M Chocolates**, 2 Cactus Garden Dr., Henderson (702/458-8864). This is where the Mars family makes its chocolates in Nevada. Kids and chocolate lovers will enjoy the free factory tour.

The factory and store are owned by the Mars chocolate empire, and only in Las Vegas can you get Mars chocolate snacks with alcohol, so watch carefully what Junior orders at the counter! There's a cactus garden adjoining the store that kids, who seem to love cacti, should find interesting and fun.

KIDD & CO. MARSHMALLOW FACTORY

These are the marshmallow pros. Near Ethel M, also in Henderson, is Kidd & Co. (8203 Gibson Rd., Henderson; 702/564-5400), a factory where the sticky, gooey stuff is made. Tours are free, and where else can you see marshmallows being made? Where else *would* you want to? Ethel M's and Kidd & Co. are a little bit of Hershey, PA, in Vegas. After the tour, a free sample is all yours - in the gift shop, of course.

14. WEDDING CHAPELS: HONEYMOON IN VEGAS

Imagine exchanging vows on a 175-foot high platform at Circus Circus, then bungee jumping to start things off with a bang. Or getting married in a helicopter, or by a singing Elvis, or in a hot tub at the back end of a stretch limo. Las Vegas is a world of extremes, and if you want to do it, you can in Vegas. Believe it or not, about five percent of all weddings in the United States take place in Las Vegas!

Last year, about 80,000 couples exchanged vows in Vegas. And Valentine's Day 1993 saw an interesting total of 2,222 marriage licenses issued, 400 more than Valentine's Day 1992. No other city can boast as many wedding chapels, nearly fifty at last count.

Actually, most chapels do not have Elvis performers or other such gimmicks. Many are of the standard, old-fashioned quickie marriage variety. Whether you're planning to tie the knot here, or just curious, take an hour or so to visit one of these chapels. It's a fun break from all the faster-paced action in Vegas.

GOING TO THE CHAPEL

State law does not require a blood test. There is no waiting period. If you're 18 years old, you're in (if you're under 18, you need a parent's or guardian's notarized consent). Just get a license from the **Clark County Mar-**

riage **License Bureau** at 200 S. 3rd Street (702/455-3156), and remember, both you and your intended have to apply in person. The license fee is $35. They're open from 8 am to midnight, Monday through Thursday, and from 8 am Friday to midnight Sunday (i.e., all weekend). If you want a Justice of the Peace and nothing fancy, walk a block to the **Commissioner of Civil Marriages**, 309 S. 3rd Street, who will get you in and out before you know it for $35.

Many chapels are grouped together at the northern end of Las Vegas Boulevard South, the bulk of them starting a short distance north of Vegas World and continuing for a ways. Mixed in among the seedier motels, pawn shops, adult video stores and less than gourmet dining, the wedding chapels of Vegas are nothing if not fun.

The biggest wedding night of the year is New Year's Eve, followed closely by Valentine's Day. As in the rest of the country, June is the biggest month. Depending on what you're looking for, you can spend as little as $100 for the whole shebang, including the license, chapel fee, minister's or judge's fee, and tip. The tip is usually about $25-50. Not a bad deal, considering the cost of weddings these days.

The better known chapels are reviewed here, with a complete list of all the wedding chapels below. Now the only remaining question is, are you *sure* you want to go through with it?

THE CHAPELS

· **Graceland Wedding Chapel**, 619 Las Vegas Blvd. S. (702/474-6655). What more could a bride and groom want? Elvis belts out a tune and serves as your witness. Fee is $45 and up. Bon Jovi got married here, and growing numbers of rockers are following his lead and are also tying the knot at this hip place. But you don't have to be a famous rock-and-roll star to get in the door here; they'll take anyone!

• **Chapel of Love**, 1431 Las Vegas Blvd. S. (702/387-0155). Very nice and never a wait; the name says it all for those romantically inclined! Four chapels are available, each with a different color scheme. What shade's for you?

• **Little Church of the West**, 3960 Las Vegas Blvd. S. (702/739-7971). Now located next door to the Hacienda Hotel on Las Vegas Boulevard South, the Little Church of the West last year celebrated its fiftieth anniversary. It used to be part of a Wild West theme park next to the Last Frontier Hotel. Free champagne.

• **Candlelight Wedding Chapel**, 2855 Las Vegas Blvd. S. (702/735-4179). Open all day and night for your marriage pleasure. Located next to the Riviera Hotel on the Strip, Candlelight is one of the most frequented wedding spots in Vegas. The chapel provides a nice touch by offering free limousine service from your hotel. Join the ranks of Bette Midler, Whoopi Goldberg, and Michael Caine by tying the knot here.

• **Chapel L'Amour**, 1901 Las Vegas Blvd. S. (702/369-5683). Both a chapel and a wedding store. If you're into red velvet, this is the place for you. They also own a long trailer called **Weddings on Wheels**, where, among other treats, you can watch the volcano blow at the Mirage Hotel while you exchange vows for richer or poorer (and as it's Vegas, the latter could be a real possibility if you don't follow Avery Cardoza's money management strategies!).

• **A Little White Chapel**, 1301 Las Vegas Blvd. S. (702/382-5493). Open 24 hours a day. The minister will come to you wherever you are, or you can motor on up or skate in to the drive-through Wedding Window and get married in the front seat (and, no doubt for some, have the honeymoon in the back seat). The likes of Demi Moore and hubby Bruce Willis, Joan Collins, and basketball great Michael Jordan have gotten hitched here. In June 1993, the folks here broke the world record for helicopter-borne marriages!

• **Las Vegas Wedding Garden.** 200 W. Sahara Avenue (702/387-0123). The chapel is a garden, offset by a lovely waterfall off to one side. Very pretty.

• **Cupid Wedding Chapel.** 1515 Las Vegas Blvd. S. (702/388-0242). Often photographed, Cupid is also one of the better known establishments. They'll make reservations for you if you're coming in from out of town.

• **Mission of the Bells**, 1213 Las Vegas Blvd. S. (702/386-1889). This is a good choice for larger weddings. The chapel is an old mission. A limousine picks you up free of charge; cake and champagne are on the house.

These are the best-known and most frequented spots, but Las Vegas's other wedding chapels may be just what you're looking for too. For other places try:
• **A-Aabel's Las Vegas Wedding Chapel**, 325 S. 3rd St. (702/382-3301)
• **A Chapel By the Courthouse**, 203 Bridger Ave. (702/384-9099)
• **Aaron's Chapel of the Bells**, 2233 Las Vegas Blvd. S. (702/735-6803)

- **All Religions Wedding Chapel**, 2855 Las Vegas Blvd. S. (702/735-4179)
- **Bally's Celebration Wedding Chapel**, 3645 Las Vegas Blvd. S., Suite 14, 702/739-4939; 800/872-1211)
- **Chapel of the Roses**, 5356 Escondido (702/387-0170)
- **Chapel of the Stars**, 2109 Las Vegas Blvd. S. (702/369-8884)
- **Circus Circus Chapel of the Fountains**, 2880 Las Vegas Blvd. S. (702/794-3777)
- **Excalibur Hotel (Canterbury Wedding Chapel)**, 3850 Las Vegas Blvd. S. (702/597-7777). Medieval wedding wear available through hotel.
- **Las Vegas Wedding and Room Coordinators**, 3909 S. Maryland Pkwy., #311-A (702/796-8697 or 800/322-VOWS)
- **Little Chapel of the Flowers**, 1717 Las Vegas Blvd. S. (702/735-4331)
- **Riviera Royale Wedding Chapel**, 2901 Las Vegas Blvd. S. (702/794-9494)
- **San Francisco Sally's Victorian Chapel**, 1304 Las Vegas Blvd. S. (702/385-7777)
- **Silver Bell Wedding Chapel**, 607 Las Vegas Blvd. S. (702/382-3726); they pay for marriage license.
- **Terry's Hitching Post Wedding Chapel**, 226 Las Vegas Blvd. S. (702/387-5080)
- **Villa Roma Wedding Chapel**, 220 Convention Center Dr. (702/731-6272)
- **Wee Kirk O' The Heather**, 231 Las Vegas Blvd. S. (702/382-9830)
- **We've Only Just Begun Wedding Chapel**, 3535 Las Vegas Blvd. S. (702/733-0011)

WHOLESALE AND RETAIL JEWELRY STORES

If you're going to get hitched, you might as well do it right and pop the question with something a trifle more valuable than a Cracker Jack's Decoder Ring. We've searched out the best bargains for you by listing both wholesalers and retail stores. Some of the better places to buy jewelry include a visit to local pawn shops, who often benefit from gamblers' need for quick cash. Try these:

- **Stoney's Loan and Jewelry**, 126 S. First St. (702/384-2686)
- **Bobby's Jewelry and Loan**, 626 Las Vegas Blvd. S. (702/382-2486)

If you want to shower your bride-to-be with unusual and exquisite American Indian jewelry, try the **Desert Indian Shop** at 108 N. Third St. (702/384-4977) or **TePee** in **Bally's Arcade** (in Bally's Hotel, 3645 Las Vegas Blvd. S.; the store's number is 702/735-5333).

If you want to spend a small fortune, look into some of the other retail jewelry stores in **Bally's Arcade,** the **Appian Way** and **Caesars Forum** at **Caesars Palace**, or the **Fashion Show Mall**. Two of Vegas's most expensive jewelry stores are located in **Caesars Forum**: **Cartier's** (702/733-6652) and **Ciro** (702/369-6464).

DIVORCE, VEGAS-STYLE

You may recall from our little history chapter that it was ol' Governor Balzar who signed Nevada's liberal wedding law back in 1931. Included in that same piece of landmark legislation was the nation's most liberal divorce law. Vegas used to be known as the Divorce Capital of America.

Getting a divorce in Las Vegas requires more staying power, but it's still breezy compared to most other states. First, become a resident for six weeks. Second, wait six weeks. Third, after the sixth week, collect your papers and you're free.

15. ARTS AND EVENTS

The calendar of annual events keeps getting more and more filled. From the rodeo to poker tournaments to crafts shows, Las Vegas has plenty of things to do all year round. The only problem you'll have is finding the time to do everything!

Here's the month-by-month breakdown on events held every year. Since the schedule for many events is subject to change, check with the folks holding the event, or the **Las Vegas Convention and Visitor's Authority** (702/892-0711) for exact days and times.

CALENDAR OF ANNUAL EVENTS

JANUARY
· Consumer Electronics Show, Las Vegas Convention Center

FEBRUARY
· Autorama Antique Car Show, Cashman Field
· Bridal Spectacular Show, Cashman Field
· Las Vegas Carnival
· Great American Train Show, Cashman Field
· LPGA (Ladies Professional Golf Association) Tournament, Desert Inn Hotel (sometimes held in March)

MARCH
- Native American Arts Festival, Clark County Heritage Museum
- Crafts Festival, Cashman Field
- St. Patrick's Day Parade and Block Party
- Hoover Dam Square Dance, Boulder City

APRIL
- Art-A-Fair and Festival of Arts, Canyon Gate Country Club
- Chamber Chorale Annual Home Concert, Artemus W. Ham Concert Hall Clark County Fair, Logandale, NV
- Henderson Industrial Days, Henderson
- World Poker Championship Series, Binion's Horseshoe Hotel (starts in April, finishes in May)
- Boulder City Spring Jamboree and Craft Show, Boulder City (sometimes held in May)

MAY
- Helldorado Days and Rodeo
- Clark County Fair and Rib Burn-Off, Sunset Park
- Clark County Artists Show, Boulder City Bicentennial Park
- JDF Monopoly Tournament (benefits Juvenile Diabetes Foundation)
- Snow Mountain Pow Wow, Las Vegas Paiute Tribe Indian Reservation (take US-95 North for 3 miles, turn at Kyle Canyon Turnoff)
- Senior Classic Golf Tournament, Desert Inn Hotel

JUNE

- Sand Bash Open Golf Tournament, Canyon Gate Country Club
- Green Valley "Concert Under the Stars" jazz show, various parks around town throughout the summer

JULY

- Fourth of July Family Pops Concert, Las Vegas Symphony Orchestra, Cashman Field
- Fourth of July Damboree, Boulder City
- Green Valley "Concert Under the Stars" classical music, Nevada Chamber Society, Green Valley Civic Center

AUGUST

- Hoedown Concert Series (bluegrass, C&W music), Jaycee Park

SEPTEMBER

- Shakespeare in the Park, Foxridge Park
- Oktoberfest, Las Vegas Art Museum
- KNPR Craftworks Market, Sunset and Athenium Drive
- Las Vegas Cup Unlimited Hydroplane Races, Lake Mead

OCTOBER

- Jaycees State Fair, either Cashman Field or the Convention Center (sometimes held in September)
- Art in the Park, Boulder City
- Fairshow, North Las Vegas (music, food, crafts, carnival)
- Las Vegas Invitational Golf Tournament, Summerlin (Tournament Players Course)

- Harvest Festival, Cashman Field (sometimes in early November)

NOVEMBER
- Antique and Classic Car Sale, Imperial Palace Hotel

DECEMBER
- Christmas Parade, Boulder City
- National Finals Rodeo, Thomas and Mack Center
- Nevada State Championship Chili Cookoff, Circus Circus
- New Year's Eve Celebration, Fremont Street, Downtown

THEATER AND MUSIC

There are several very good theater companies in Las Vegas, outside the big production shows at the major hotels. The **Charleston Heights Arts Center** (901 Brush St.; 702/229-6383) is home to the **New West Stage Company**. The **Clark County Library** (1401 E. Flamingo; 702/647-7469) is the venue for the city and regional theater companies that seem to come and go. Two of the better-known and critically acclaimed troupes that perform here are the **Actor's Repertory Theater**, and the **Las Vegas Chamber Orchestra** (for those of you with more high-brow tastes).

The **Repertory Theater** and the **Nevada Dance Theater** can be seen at UNLV's **Judy Bayley Theater** (702/739-3801). The Repertory Theater puts on a variety of new plays and old standards. For opera buffs, the **Nevada Opera Theater** (702/737-6373) is the main game in town at the **Artemus W. Ham Concert Hall**. For summer outdoor thespian fans, **Spring Mountain Ranch** outside of Vegas puts on **Theater Under the Stars**, which is a very enjoyable way to spend a mid-summer night's eve. Call the ranch at 702/875-4141 to find out what's playing when you'll be in town.

CONVENTIONS

Vegas is host to an amazing number of conventions. Most are held at the Convention Center, but quite a few hotels have sizable convention floor space and hold their share of big meetings too. The Convention Center has a number of conventions booked through the year 2005!

Some of the big shows, like the annual Consumer Electronics Show held each January, attract anywhere from 80,000 to 100,000 conventioneers. There is a broad diversity of shows, from the American Ostrich Association to the Casino Chips and Gaming Tokens Collectors Club.

From humble beginnings in 1959, the Las Vegas Convention Center now measures 1.3 million square feet. About two million people came to Las Vegas' numerous conventions last year. For information about facilities or bookings, call or write the Las Vegas Convention Center, 3150 Paradise Rd., Las Vegas, NV 89109 (702/892-0711).

INDEX

The Cardoza Craps Master - Three Big Strategies!

Exclusive Offer! - Not Available Anywhere Else

Here It is! **At last**, the **secrets** of the **Grande-Gold Power Sweep, Molliere's Monte Carlo Turnaround** and the **Montarde-D'Girard Double Reverse** - three big strategies - are made available and presented for the **first time anywhere**! These powerful strategies are designed for the serious craps player, one wishing to bring the best odds and strategies to hot, cold and choppy tables.

1. The Grande-Gold Power Sweep (Hot Table Strategy)

This **dynamic strategy** takes maximum advantage of hot tables and shows the player methods of amassing small **fortunes quickly** when numbers are being thrown fast and furious. The Grande-Gold stresses aggressive betting on wagers the house has no edge on! This previously unreleased strategy will make you a powerhouse at a hot table.

2. Molliere's Monte Carlo Turnaround (Cold Table Strategy)

For the player who likes betting against the dice, **Molliere's Monte Carlo** Turnaround shows how to turn a cold table into hot cash. Favored by an exclusive circle of professionals who will play nothing else, the uniqueness of this strongman strategy is that the vast majority of bets **give absolutely nothing away to the casino**!

3. The Montarde-D'Girard Double Reverse (Choppy Table Strategy)

This **new** strategy is the **latest development** and the **most exciting strategy** to be designed in recent years. **Learn how** to play the optimum strategies when the dice run hot and cold (a choppy table) with no apparent reason. **The Montarde-d'Girard Double Reverse** shows you how you can **generate big profits** while less knowledgeable players are ground out by choppy dice. And, of course, the majority of our bets give nothing away to the casino!

BONUS!!! - Order now, and receive **The Craps Master-Professional Money Management Formula** ($15 value) **absolutely free**! Necessary for serious players and **used by the pros**, it features the unique **stop-loss ladder.**

To order send $75 $50 by check or money order to: <u>Cardoza Publishing</u>

Win at Blackjack Without Counting Cards!
Breakthrough in Blackjack!!!
The Cardoza 1,2,3 Non-Counter Strategy

BEAT MULTIPLE DECK BLACKJACK WITHOUT COUNTING CARDS!
You heard right! Now, for the **first time** ever, **win** at multiple deck blackjack **without counting cards**! Until I developed the Cardoza Multiple Deck Non-Counter (The 1,2,3 Strategy), I thought it was impossible. Don't be intimidated anymore by 4, 6 or 8 deck games - for now you have the **advantage**!

EXCITING STRATEGY - ANYONE CAN WIN!
We're **excited** about this strategy for it allows anyone at all to **have the advantage** over any casino in the world in a multiple deck game. You don't need a great memory, you don't need to count cards, you don't need to be good at math - you only need to know the **winning secrets** of the Cardoza Multiple Deck Non-Counter and use but a **little effort** to be a **winner**.

SIMPLE BUT EFFECTIVE - BE A LEISURELY WINNER!
This strategy is so **simple**, yet so **effective**, you will be amazed. With a **minimum of effort**, this remarkable strategy, which we also call the 1,2,3 (as easy as 1,2,3), allows you to **win** without studiously following cards. Drink, converse, whatever - they'll never suspect that you can **beat the casino**!

Not as powerful as a card counting strategy, but **powerful enough to make you a winner** - with the odds!!!

EXTRA BONUS!
Complete listing of all options and variations at blackjack and how they affect the player. ($5 Value!) **Extra, Extra Bonus!!** Not really a bonus for we could not sell you the strategy without protecting you against getting barred. The 1,000 word essay, "How to Disguise the Fact That You're an Expert," and 1,500 word "How Not To Get Barred," are also included free. ($15 Value)

To Order, send ~~$75~~ $50 by check or money order to <u>Cardoza Publishing</u>

ABOUT THE AUTHORS

Ed Kranmar is a travel writer and publisher who has trekked the length and breadth of the Southwest, frequently for long stays in Vegas. He often accompanies Cardoza on his trips to the desert gambling mecca, studying the constantly changing Las Vegas scene to bring you an up-to-date, insiders' perspective.

Avery Cardoza is the best-selling author of many how-to-win gaming books and advanced strategies, and is recognized as one of the top gambling authorities in the world. He is also head of Cardoza Publishing, the world's foremost publisher of gambling books. Cardoza, a former resident of Las Vegas, has spent many years in the world's greatest gambling city conducting extensive research into the mathematical, emotional, and psychological aspects of winning.

FROM THE PUBLISHERS

Our goal is to provide you with a guide book second to none. Please bear in mind, however, that things change: phone numbers, admission price, addresses, etc. Should you come across any new information, we'd appreciate hearing from you. No item is too small for us, so if you have a great recommendation, find an error, see that some place has gone out of business, or just plain disagree with our recommendations, write to:

Ed Kranmar and Avery Cardoza
c/o Open Road Publishing
P.O. Box 11249
Cleveland Park Station
Washington, DC 20008